JOY OF LIVING BIBLE STUDY SERIES

DRINKING
FROM THE
LIVING WELL

Studies in John 1–11

Practical Studies for Personal Growth
DORIS W. GREIG

Regal Books

A Division of GL Publications
Ventura, California, U.S.A.

Other Titles in the Regal
"Joy of Living" Series

Courage to Conquer (Daniel)
Living in the Light (1, 2, 3 John and Jude)
Power for Positive Living (Philippians and Colossians)
Walking in God's Way (Ruth and Esther)
Exercising a Balanced Faith (James)
Discovering God's Power (Genesis 1-17)
Discovering God's Promises (Genesis 18-31)

Published by Regal Books
A Division of GL Publications
Ventura, California 93006
Printed in U.S.A.

Library of Congress Cataloging-in-Publication Data applied for

1 2 3 4 5 6 7 8 9 10 / 91 90 89

Rights for publishing this book in other languages are contracted by Gospel Literature International (GLINT) foundation. GLINT also provides technical help for the adaptation, translation, and publishing of Bible study resources and books in scores of languages worldwide. For further information, contact GLINT, Post Office Box 488, Rosemead, California, 91770, U.S.A., or the publisher.

CONTENTS

How to Get the Most from this Book   5

The key verse of the book of John is usually considered to be John 20:31. "That you may believe that Jesus is the Christ, the son of God."

In the original Greek, the word "miracle" could be translated "sign." The Lord Jesus began to work miracles in Cana.

God's gift of love to the world was His only begotten Son (John 3:16). Yet the giving of this gift does not make it yours.

It was Jesus Christ Himself who gave women a place of honor in society. As they came to Him for forgiveness of their sins, they became joint heirs with Jesus Christ (through their faith).

The Pharisees had examined the Bible carefully and knew of its many details, yet they did not realize that the most important purpose for it was to point them to the Messiah, Jesus Christ.

To believe is more than just to know something is true; to believe is to act upon what we know is true.

Those who enjoy the indwelling Holy Spirit, a well of "living water," have a reservoir which can cause their lips to overflow with kind and gracious words of blessing.

HOW TO GET THE MOST FROM THIS BOOK

The Bible is a living book! It is relevant and powerful, but more than that, it is the active voice of our living God, and He wants to communicate with you daily through His Word. As you study the Bible, you will learn about God's person and character. You will begin to find His purpose for your life as He speaks to you through His written Word. His purpose is unchanging and His principles are unfailing guidelines for living. He will show us His truth and what our response should be to it.

Will you set aside a special time each day to interact with God in His Word? As you read, study, meditate and memorize His Word, the Holy Spirit will guide you, and His direction for your life will be made clear. More and more, His voice will be easily discerned in the din of life's pressures. When your heart is available and you see God's good intentions for you, you will then learn how to respond to the Lord's personal call to you day by day, moment by moment. As you train your ears to hear the voice of God, you will recognize His presence in the most unlikely circumstances and places. "The grass withers and the flowers fall, but the word of our God stands forever" (Isaiah 40:8, *NIV*).

Try to have several versions of the Bible available as you study. Comparing these versions will enrich your understanding of a passage and bring added insight. Try not to use a commentary or any other reference work until you have allowed the Lord to speak personally to you through His Word.

Each lesson begins with a section of *Study Notes*. After Lesson 1, the introductory lesson, these Notes suggest ways to understand the passage at hand and relate it to other biblical teaching. Following the *Study Notes* is a section of *Questions,* designed to guide your Bible study through a six-day week. On the first day you review the previous Notes. And Days 2-6 will prepare you for the next lesson. You will benefit most from your study if you will do each day's questions at a regular time.

This study is designed to be used individually or in a group. If you are studying in a group, we urge you to actively share your answers and thoughts. In sharing we give encouragement to others and learn from one another.

This book has been conveniently hole-punched and perforated for easy tearout and insertion in a 6″ × 9½″ looseleaf notebook:

- Bible study pages lie flat in your notebook for ease of writing as you study.

- Additional notebook paper can be inserted for journaling or more extensive notes and other relevant information.

- Additional studies in the Joy of Living Series can be inserted, along with your personal notes, and tabbed to help you build your Bible study file for easy, future reference.

May God bless you as you begin your journey into His Word. This may be the first time for you to take this trip, or it may be that you have journeyed this way many times before. No matter what trip it is for you, we pray you will find new joy and hope as you seek to live in the light of the living God!

INTRODUCTION TO THE GOSPEL OF JOHN

Study Notes

The Sourcebook for Our Study

We are about to begin a study of the book of John, but we will be searching other books of the Bible as we seek to understand John's Gospel.

The Bible is a single library of 66 books; *His Story, God's Story.* The Old and New Testaments mesh together to give us God's complete Word. The Bible contains 66 books written by 40 authors, as the Holy Spirit inspired them and it was all recorded over a period of 1,600 years.

The Old Testament was recorded in the Hebrew language with a few short passages in Aramaic. Then about 100 years before Christ's appearance on the earth, it was translated into the Greek language. The New Testament was also recorded in Greek. Our translations have all come from these original languages.

The books of the Bible were written by divinely chosen men in known and existing languages and were accepted as God's Word by the people of that generation because these books possessed certain qualities which instinctively showed the believers of that day that they were from God. During the period that followed the death of the apostles, many books appeared that were claimed to have been written by them. While these books never gained universal acceptance, they did bring some confusion to the early Christians. For that reason a church council, toward the close of the fourth century, laid down a number of rules by which every book claiming inspiration would be measured.

A book had to meet many requirements. Among other things it was necessary (1) that an apostle had either written it or confirmed it; (2) that it had enjoyed universal acceptance from apostolic days; (3) that it had been read in all the churches; and (4) that it had been recognized by the church fathers as inspired.

After careful examination it was determined that the New Testament books met the requirements. These 27 New Testament books distinctly bore the marks of inspiration and Divine authority. Most of them were completed before A.D. 80. This is a significant fact because the time of their writing confirms that the events recorded in the New Testament are the actual historical events of Christ's life on earth and the early Church.

"For the word of God is quick, and powerful, and sharper than any twoedged sword, piercing even to the dividing asunder of soul and spirit, and of the joints and marrow, and is a discerner of the thoughts and intents of the heart" (Hebrews 4:12). This is a remarkable and astounding claim which God the Holy Spirit, the Author of our Bible, makes for the Word of God, the Bible. Truly the Bible is a book of all other books and has been appropriately called "The Book of Books." It is often referred to as "God's Miracle Book" not only because it records many miracles within its pages, many supernatural acts of the Living God, but also because its very existence and nature are a marvel!

No other book in the history of the world has ever been so vigorously and universally attacked. Down through the centuries men have tried their best to exterminate it, to wipe out its very existence, and to discredit the written Word of God in every way possible. Yet in spite of all its enemies and critics, the Bible has seen their defeat and frustration!

It was none other than the Frenchman, Voltaire, who said in the last part of the eighteenth century, that within 100 years the Bible and all Christianity would be completely forgotten. Voltaire died in 1778, but since that time the world has been flooded with millions upon millions of Bibles in scores of languages, dialects, and tongues.

An ironic footnote to history is the fact that, within 25 years of Voltaire's death in 1778, his own printing press—from which had come his denunciations of the Word of God—was being used to print copies of the Bible. And the very house where he had lived became a Bible storehouse for the Geneva Bible Society. God, not Voltaire, indeed had the last word!

The Bible's history reminds one of a man who built a wall six feet wide and four feet tall. When he was asked why he built the wall wider than it was high his reply was, "So that when the enemy thinks that he is destroying the wall by tipping it over, he'll only find it stands higher than it was before!" One might as well try to keep the sun from rising as to attempt to stop the onward march of the Bible as men around the world seek to find out God's message from it.

> *The Bible portrays Jesus Christ as Savior and Lord . . . . It is amazing that 40 authors over a period of 1,600 years should have this one theme portrayed in all of their writings.*

No other book has survived this length of time with such *a unity of purpose!* The Bible portrays Jesus Christ as Savior and Lord for any who will believe and receive Him. It is amazing that 40 authors over a period of 1,600 years should have this one theme portrayed in all of their writings. How is this possible? Only as the Spirit of God moved in their hearts and led them to write God's written revelation of Himself could this ever have happened.

This book, the Bible, is like a ship that has managed to sail down the river of time safely preserved by God's own hand. Other books have set sail at nearly the same time and have joined the Bible in this sail down the river of time. Some of these books have been shipwrecked in various ways and lost. Others have completely disappeared without our ever having known that they existed. But this is not true of God's Word to us, the Bible. It has sailed safely down this river of time all the way to us in this present generation.

Why has the Bible had such a safe journey? Why has it not suffered a shipwreck or a quiet harbor death? Because it is God's personal message to us. He has preserved this message in the book we call the Holy Bible. He wanted us to know His love for us, and His plan for each of our lives. He preserved the book which shows us this love and these plans for each person He created.

Our basic text for this study is the Gospel of John in the New Testament. You will need an Old Testament also, as the two testaments are inseparably intertwined in their message to us. We suggest that you use not only a King James Bible, but also a modern language translation, particularly if you are new to Bible study.

Among these translations are the *Revised Standard Version,* the *New American Standard Bible,* the *Amplified Bible,* or the paraphrase, *The Living Bible. We would suggest that you underline favorite verses in your Bible as you find them.* If you are a Roman Catholic, you will enjoy reading and comparing the *Douay* with the *New Jerusalem Bible,* and the Roman Catholic edition of the Living Bible. These

Bibles are all approved by the Catholic Church.

You will be interested that the word "testament" means a covenant, an agreement and a promise. The Old Testament is the covenant promise that God made with man about His salvation. (Look up salvation in the dictionary.) This was before the Lord Jesus Christ came to earth. The New Testament is the agreement which God made with man after the Lord Jesus Christ came to earth.

The Old Covenant or promise stated simply was that God required a sacrifice to be made for sin in anticipation of the Messiah. Therefore the plan was that the priest by faith in God's promise would kill the lamb in the temple for sin offering and present the blood for the forgiveness of the sins of the people.

The New Covenant is that the Lord Jesus Christ in fulfillment of God's promise came to earth as the Lamb of God and shed His blood for sin. "For this is my blood of the new testament, which is shed for many for the remission of sins" (Matthew 26:28—the Lord Jesus Christ's own words). "Behold the Lamb of God, which taketh away the sin of the world" (John 1:29—John the Baptist's words concerning the Lord Jesus Christ).

God Speaks Through the Bible

The Bible speaks primarily of God and secondarily of man. God is the subject of the Bible; man the loving object! The Bible tells us of what God has done and what man has received. It speaks of God's glory, creation, power, love, grace (*G*od's *R*iches *A*t *C*hrist's *E*xpense), mercy, judgment, goodness and patience. The Bible reveals to us that God is love! "The heavens declare the glory of God; and the firmament sheweth his handywork. Day unto day uttereth speech, and night unto night sheweth knowledge" (Psalm 19:1-2).

The words of the Lord in the Bible are "more to be desired . . . than gold, yea, than much fine gold: sweeter also than honey and the honeycomb" (Psalm 19:10). We might compare the Word of God to a uranium mine that gives up the precious metal only after careful searching. If you are willing to search the Bible through this daily study plan and obey them, you'll discover the precious promises of God which are better than "fine gold; sweeter also than honey and the honeycomb!"

The amazing story is told of what happened on Pitcairn Island. Perhaps you remember the true story of *Mutiny on the Bounty*. After the mutineers scuttled the *Bounty*, some British sailors, some native men and women and a few children went ashore on Pitcairn Island. It was not long before one of the sailors discovered a way of distilling alcohol, and soon Pitcairn Island became a veritable hell of drunkenness, vice and murder.

One day Alexander Smith, while rummaging through one of the ship's old trunks earlier brought ashore from the *Bounty*, found a Bible. He began to read it and his life was changed by Jesus Christ. He began to read it to the others and their lives were changed.

Years later, when the United States ship, the *Topaz*, landed at Pitcairn Island they found a community of Christian people! It was a community without drunkenness, without profanity, a place where God was worshipped and where His commandments were obeyed. It was a model Christian community, all the result of the finding and reading of the Word of God, the Bible, which revealed Jesus Christ as Savior and Lord.

In any society, God speaks to men and women through the Bible. A chieftain in a Fiji Island, said to a visitor, "Do you see that rock over there? That's where we crushed the skulls of our captives in past generations. Do you see that place over there? That's where we built our fire and roasted our victims. Had it not been for the missionaries coming to us with the Bible, you wouldn't get off this island alive. Your head would be crushed. You would be roasted, and my people would serve you at a banquet!"

The Bible has transformed lives of drunkards and drug addicts in our society. It has turned cannibals into peaceful men with a respect for human life. It has changed atheists into humble believers and followers of the Lord Jesus Christ. Even people of wealth and position, who have "everything" yet "nothing," have found faith and purpose in Jesus Christ. Jesus Christ has entered the lives of desperately unhappy people to give meaning, purpose, and a blessedness to their lives that they never dreamed possible. As the Bible reveals the Lord Jesus Christ to us, we discover our peace and joy in Him. "Look around and be distressed; look within and be depressed; look to Jesus and be at rest!" (Corrie ten Boom)

Introduction to John's Gospel

Now for a little background on the Gospel of John before we begin our study. John portrays Jesus Christ as the Son of God. He refers to himself as the disciple whom Jesus loved . . . who has written these things (John 21:20,24). John also refers to himself in John 13:23; 19:26; 20:2; and 21:7, although he does not identify himself by name in these Scriptures. The early writers who speak of the Gospel of John identify the author as "the beloved disciple," the apostle John, the son of Zebedee.

11

Mark 1:19-20 gives us information about John's family. John, his father, Zebedee, and his brother James, were fishermen on the lake of Galilee and were partners of Simon Peter (Luke 5:10). The two brothers were called "Boanerges" meaning "sons of thunder" by Jesus in Mark 3:17. It is believed that their mother was Salome (Mark 15:40; Matthew 27:56).

John referring to himself in this Gospel, is with Peter in every instance except at the cross in John 19:26. After Pentecost, John was associated with Peter in Jerusalem (Acts 3:1-4) and also on the Samaritan missions (Acts 8:14-25). Paul spoke of John as one of the three "pillar" apostles that he saw on his visit to Jerusalem after he became a Christian (Galatians 2:9-10).

John states that the purpose of his book is to show that Jesus was the Christ, the promised Messiah (for the Jews), and the Son of God (for the Gentiles), and to lead believers into a life of spiritual friendship with Him. The theme of John's Gospel is the deity of Christ.

John states that the purpose of his book is to show that Jesus was the Christ, the promised Messiah (for the Jews), and the Son of God (for the Gentiles), and to lead believers into a life of spiritual friendship with Him. This is stated firmly in the first 18 verses of John called the Prologue.

The theme of John's Gospel is the deity of Christ. More here than anywhere else His divine Sonship is set forth. In this Gospel we are shown that the "Babe of Bethlehem" was none other than the "only begotten of the Father" (see John 1:18; John 3:16; 1 John 4:9).

John gives evidences that "all things were made by Him," "in Him was life, yet he was made flesh and dwelt among us." No man could see God; therefore Christ came to reveal Him. This is the message of the book of John. John gives significant titles to the Lord Jesus Christ in this book. Only here He is called "the Word." John also calls the Lord Jesus Christ the Creator, the only begotten of the Father, the Lamb of God and the revelation of the great "I AM" (Exodus 3:14).

John may have been about 25 years of age when Jesus called him. He had been a follower of John the Baptist. In the reign of the Roman emperor Domitian, John the Disciple was banished to Patmos, but afterward he returned to Ephesus and became the pastor of that wonderful church. He lived in Ephesus to an old age of about 96, the last

12

of the twelve apostles. During this time he wrote his Gospel concerning the deity of Christ, co-eternal with the Father.

John wrote nearly a generation after the other evangelists, somewhere between A.D. 80 and 100. All of the other New Testament books had been completed except for his own writings. The life and work of Jesus was well known at this time. The gospel had been preached, Paul and Peter had suffered martyrdom, all the apostles had died, Jerusalem had been destroyed by the Roman legions under Titus, A.D. 70 and Matthew, Mark and Luke were written.

Already false teachers had arisen denying that Jesus Christ was the Son of God come in the flesh. John, therefore, wrote emphasizing those truths and gave the names of the witnesses, and recorded the words and works of Jesus that revealed His divine power and glory. Matthew portrays the Lord Jesus Christ as "Son of David" and Luke portrays Him as "Son of man." In John, He is portrayed as "Son of God."

The Lord Jesus Christ's deity is emphasized by John. Jesus is shown dwelling with God before the Creation (John 1:1-2). He is called "the only begotten of the Father" (John 1:14). He is called the "Son of God" (John 1:34). Jesus speaks of God as "my Father" 35 times in the book of John. Speaking with authority He says "Verily, verily" 35 times.

Unlocking John's Gospel

Dr. F.D. Gordon suggests, "There are three keys that unlock John's Gospel." The "Back Door Key" is John 20:31, "But these are written, that ye might believe that Jesus is the Christ, the Son of God; and that believing ye might have life through his name."

The "Side Door Key" is John 16:28. At the Last Supper with His disciples, Jesus reveals this truth to them: "I came forth from the Father, and am come into the world: again, I leave the world, and go to the Father." His constant thought was that He used to be with the Father. He came down to earth on an errand and stayed for 33 years. He would go back again to His Father.

The "Front Door Key" is John 1:12. *This key hangs right at the very front, outside, low down, within every person's reach!* "But as many as received him, to them gave he power to become the sons of God, even to them that believe on his name." *This is the Great Key—the Chief Key to the whole house. Its use permits the front door to be flung wide open. Anyone who believes may enter!*

And so we open the book of John with this question—"What do you think of Christ?" Is He only the world's greatest teacher or is He actually God? Was He one of the prophets, or is He the world's Savior whose coming was foretold by the prophets?

You may have some of these questions in your own mind. We suggest that you bring your doubts one by one to the Lord Jesus Christ as you study the Bible, and one by one God will deal with your questions through His Holy Spirit as you study and obey His Word, the Bible. You will begin to realize that Christ is a living Person, though invisible. As you trust Him, you will begin to experience His love for you and His desire to help you in your life here on earth, as well as His promise to give to you the gift of eternal life as you trust Him as your Lord and Savior (see John 3:16,17).

Ask yourself this question now: "What shall I sacrifice this week in time, so that I may spend time with God? *Make a daily appointment with God.* Find a quiet spot. Take your Bible, pencil or pen and your lesson with you. If you have a busy phone, you may have to remove it from the hook, lower the bell tone or hide the phone under a blanket to muffle the ringing!

Remember your appointment with God is more important than your annual dental checkup and you wouldn't dream of missing that. *Keep your appointment with God daily.* Pray now and ask God the following things:

1. How many minutes do I want to give to the Lord each day?
2. What do I need to sacrifice to give the Lord this time? Examples: sleep, television, casual telephone conversations, window shopping, etc. Each person will have to decide what her priorities are and what can be removed from the daily schedule to give time to God.
3. What is my *best time* for my appointment with God?
4. Where is the quietest place for me to pray and study?
5. Do I really want to spend time with God? If your last answer is yes, God will bless you as you work out the time. If your last answer is no, pray that God will give you a desire, a hunger to have this time with Him. He will do this for you!

Study Questions

Before you begin your study this week:

1. Pray each day and ask God to speak to you through His Holy Spirit.
2. Use only your Bible to answer the following questions.
3. Write down your answers and, where called for, include the verses you used.
4. Challenge questions are for those who have the time and who wish to do them.
5. Personal questions are to be shared with your study group only if you wish to share.
6. As you study, look for a verse to memorize this week. Write it down, carry it with you, tack it to your bulletin board, tape it to the dashboard of your car. Make a real effort to learn the verse and its reference.

FIRST DAY: Read all of the preceding notes and look up all of the Scriptures given.

1. What was one new thought for you in the notes?

2. What was the most meaningful Scripture from the notes to you personally?

3. (Personal) Have you chosen to take up the challenge to give daily time to this study and to God? What sacrifice has God shown you that you could make to give time to Him in study and prayer? (Share if possible with your group, as it may help someone else.)

SECOND DAY: Read all of John 1 concentrating on verses 1-5.

Note: Comparing John 1:14 with John 1:1 you will discover that "the Word became flesh and dwelt among us." Thus the "Word" is the Lord Jesus Christ.

1 a. What does John 1:1 tell you about the Lord Jesus Christ?

   b. What part of John 1:1 is repeated in John 1:2 and why do you think it is repeated?

   c. Who created all things? Give verse.

2. **Challenge:** What does Genesis 1:26 say which confirms what John 1:1-2 says about the Word, the Lord Jesus Christ?

3. What do the following verses say concerning the Lord Jesus Christ? Put the verses into your own words if you wish to.

   Colossians 1:16-17

   1 John 1:1

4. How does John 1:4 emphasize what the Lord Jesus said about Himself in John 14:6? What significant word do you find in both verses?

5 a. What does the Lord Jesus say about Himself in John 8:12?

   b. (Personal) Do you have the "light of life?" A person receives this "light of life" by receiving the Lord Jesus Christ by faith. See Titus 3:5.

c. What does Acts 4:12 say that emphasizes what the Lord Jesus said in John 14:6?

6. Challenge: What do you believe John 1:5 means?

THIRD DAY: Read John 1:6-14.

1 **a.** Who was the man sent from God?

 b. Why did God send him? Give verses.

2. How does John 1:10 reemphasize John 1:3 and John 1:5?

3. Challenge: What do you believe John 1:11 means?

4. To those who are willing to receive Jesus Christ, what power is given according to John 1:12?

5. (Personal) Have you ever received this power? See 1 John 5:13. What does it say concerning belief?

6 **a.** What new or important things do you learn about the Lord Jesus Christ in John 1:14?

b. **Challenge:** If you do not know what the word grace means in John 1:14, look it up in a dictionary or a Bible dictionary. What do you believe God's grace means?

FOURTH DAY: Read John 1:15-28.

1 a. What was given by Moses? Give verse.

b. Challenge: What does Hebrews 10:1-4 say concerning the law? Summarize these verses in your own words if possible.

c. What was offered once and for all time for our sins according to Hebrews 10:10?

2. What was given by Jesus Christ? (See John 1:15-28.)

3. What special place did the Lord Jesus have with the Father before He came to earth as the God-man to bring us truth and grace? Give verse in John 1.

4. How did John compare himself to Jesus Christ when the religious leaders questioned him? Give verse.

5. **Challenge:** How do the following verses describe Christ as Ruler and King over all humanity? Try to put them into your own words.

Philippians 2:9-11

1 Peter 3:22

6 a. (Personal) Have you received the Lord Jesus not only as Savior but as the Lord and King of your life?

  b. How do you believe a person can allow Jesus Christ to be the Lord and King of his life? See John 12:26 and Romans 12:2 to help you think about this question.

FIFTH DAY: Read John 1:29-34.

1. When John saw the Lord Jesus, how did he describe Him?

2. How does John describe how he saw the Spirit descend on Jesus Christ? Give verse.

3. What did John baptize with and what does the Lord Jesus baptize with?

4. What do the following verses say concerning the Holy Ghost (Holy Spirit)? Put them into your own words if possible.

1 Corinthians 12:13

Ephesians 1:13

5. How does Romans 14:17 describe the Kingdom of God?

6. What other name does John give to Jesus Christ in John 1:34?

SIXTH DAY: Read John 1:35-51.

1 a. What did John the Baptist call the Lord Jesus again in John 1:36 that he had already called Him in John 1:29?

b. What was the result of John's words about Jesus Christ? Give verse.

c. What invitation did Jesus extend to these two?

d. What was the name of one of these men?

2 a. What did Andrew do after he had met the Lord Jesus Christ?

b. (Personal) Have you ever followed the Lord Jesus Christ by faith as Andrew did? Have you gone out to tell someone else about Him as Andrew did?

c. What are ways a person could introduce someone to Jesus Christ today?

3. What new name did the Lord Jesus give to Simon, and what other facts did He give about Simon which shows that He knew all about him before Andrew brought him? Give verse please.

4 a. Whom did Jesus call to follow Him in John 1:43?

b. Whom did Philip go tell about the Lord Jesus? What did he tell this person about Him? Give verse.

c. What did the Lord Jesus say to Nathanael that showed Christ already knew all about him before He saw him? Give verses.

5. How did Nathanael declare his faith in the Lord Jesus? Give verse.

6 a. **Challenge:** These men had recognized Jesus as the Messiah whom Moses and the other prophets had written about. How do the following verses from the Old Testament foretell the coming of the Lord Jesus?

Jeremiah 23:5

Job 19:25

b. Which thought or Scripture verse in this lesson was the most helpful or challenging to you? Will you memorize a verse which will help you to remember this special challenge or thought?

THAT YOU MAY BELIEVE

John 1

Study Notes

Introduction

When you open your Bible to the New Testament and discover Gospels by Matthew, Mark and Luke, do you wonder why John felt that he should write another Gospel of the life of Christ? As you study the Gospel of John you will see that John wrote for a reason different than the other Gospel writers.

Matthew was written especially to the Jews: here Christ is presented as the "son of David" (Jeremiah 23:5; Matthew 1:1; Matthew 21:9; Isaiah 11:1-10; Jeremiah 33:15). Mark was written to the Romans, who were interested in what a person did: here Christ is presented as the "servant of the Lord". Mark includes an account of more miracles than any of the other Gospels. There is no genealogy in Mark, for who cares where a servant came from! Luke wrote to the Greeks, who were interested in the ideal man: here the Lord Jesus is presented as the "perfect man" and His genealogy is traced all the way to Adam.

The Lord Jesus Christ is the central figure of each of the four Gospels. Each writer presents Him with a different emphasis, but Christ is the subject of each one. John wrote to all people to present the deity of Christ in his Gospel. *Christ is God!* This is the proclamation of John's Gospel. No one but Christ could ever be shown as John chose to present his Lord. *Only Christ is God!* John wanted us to know this truth.

The key verse of the book of John is usually considered to be John 20:31. This is why the book of John was written. "That you may believe that Jesus is the Christ, the Son of God." When you believe in Christ something happens: "Believing ye may have life in his name." Jesus stated that He was life, and the only way to the Father in John 14:6. "I am the way, the truth, and the life: no man cometh unto the Father, but by me." He also spoke of the abundant life that He wanted to give each one who came to Him by simple faith. "I am come that they might have life, and that they might have it more abundantly" (John 10:10). Do you have an abundant life because you have received the Lord Jesus Christ by faith?

We know that to be in the center of God's will is to be in the center of God's abundant life for us! Are you willing to be still and know that He is God?

Elisabeth Elliot started her mission work in South America as a single woman along with three other single women. There was no church, no believers, and no male missionaries. Later she became a wife and had to rearrange certain priorities in her life in accordance with the mission field of her co-worker husband, and again later as a mother. When her husband was killed by the Auca Indians, she found herself in a difficult position. Not one male missionary was left in Ecuador at that time who spoke the Quichua language. No one was there to teach the young Quichua Christians and or to lead the church. Only one woman was left to carry on where five missionary men had left off. The door to the Auca tribe had slammed shut.

Yet that same door was opened to two women, to their total astonishment. One was Rachel Saint, the sister of Nate Saint, one of the missionary men who was killed, and the other was Elisabeth Elliot. It didn't look like a woman's job, but God's categories are not always ours! For eight years she did missionary work among the Quichua Christians. Then she came back to the United States to become a wife and homemaker once again. She was widowed for a second time, and has since remarried. This woman knows the "abundant life." The following is her statement after all of these experiences: "But it is the same faithful Lord who called me by name and never loses track of my goings and reminds us all in a still, small voice, 'Ye are my witnesses that ye might know and believe me and understand that I am he.' There's our primary responsibility; to know Him. I can't be a witness unless I've seen something, unless I know what it is I am to testify to."

Elisabeth goes on to say that the Lord of the Universe who calls you offers you a place in His program. Your education or lack of it, your taste, prejudices, fears, ambitions, age, sex, color, height, marital status or income bracket are all things which may be offered to God, after you've presented your body as a living sacrifice (Romans 12:1). "And God knows exactly what to do with them. They're not obstacles if you hand them over. Be still and know that He is God."

Sit in silence and wonder in expectancy, and never doubt that the Lord of your life has His own way of getting through to you to let you know the specifics of His will. We know that to be in the center of God's will is to be in the center of God's abundant life for us! Are you willing to be still and know that He is God?

The Gospel of John was written several years after the first three Gospels were completed, probably between A.D. 90 and 100. The author was John the Apostle, the beloved disciple, the son of Zebedee. Along with his brother, James, and with Peter, John belonged to the inner circle of disciples. This was a group near to Christ at such occasions as the Transfiguration and in the Garden of Gethsemane.

This intimate knowledge of Jesus Christ's life gives a special flavor to all that John writes. He knew the high priest personally at the time of the trial of Jesus Christ (John 18:15). He could tell the distance between Jerusalem and Bethany (John 11:18). His friendship with Christ is seen in the last detailed discourse of the Lord (John 14—16), and the intercessory prayer of the Lord in John 17. In the last two verses of the Gospel of John, he tells us he is willing to stand behind his testimony, and that he could have told much, much more!

The book is often called "The Gospel of the Son of God." It is divided into five parts.

1. The Prologue—John 1:1-18

2. Christ's Public Ministry—John 1:19—12:50

3. His Private Ministry—John 13—17

4. His Glorification—John 18—20

5. Postscript—John 21:1-25

The key word of the Gospel is "believe" which John used in some form 101 times. This is twice as often as all of the other three Gospels combined! John filled his book with special names and titles of Christ. Here are some of the titles which we find in John: The Word (John 1:1), the Lamb of God (1:29), the only begotten Son of God (3:16), the Bread of Life (6:35), the Light of the World (8:12), the "I AM" (8:58), the Good Shepherd (10:11), the Resurrection (11:25), the Way, the Truth, and the Life (14:6), and the Vine (15:1).

The Lord Jesus Christ—The Word
John 1:1-18

In John 1:1 we find a new title for Christ; He is called the Word. A word is an expression of an idea or a thought. We cannot know what someone is thinking until he puts his thoughts into words! Jesus Christ shows us what God is. Jesus Himself said, "If ye had known me, ye should have known my Father also: and from henceforth ye know him, and have seen him . . . . he that hath seen me hath seen the Father" (John 14:7-9). Jesus Christ is the personal revelation of God; He is the Word. This first verse also tells us that Jesus Christ is God! In Hebrews 1:3 we read that Jesus Christ is "the express image of his person."

In John 1:2 we discover that Jesus Christ is eternal! There was never a place in all of eternity in which the Son of God was not present. Nobody made Him; He always has been. Christ is also the creator of all things (John 1:3). This is again reemphasized in John 1:10.

From these verses we conclude that the Lord Jesus Christ was the Word of God made flesh. He was eternal, preexistent, and then became flesh to reveal God to us. Christ existed before the world was created. Christ was with God (John 1:1) and in communion with Him throughout all time. The Lord Jesus Christ was God and thus is identical in power with God the Father.

John spoke of Jesus' miracles as signs. Jesus was simply opening windows to the reality of His power as a person of the Trinity. The Lord Jesus Christ did these miracles to show "the glory of God" (John 11:4). He had love and compassion in the miracles. Every miracle revealed the glory of God as He participated in human affairs.

If the Christian is to have an abundant life he should have a "quiet hour." There is a "quiet hour" for industry also! If you were to go into the office of Steelcase, an office furniture factory, between 7:30-8:30 A.M., the silence would be deafening. This Toronto company has decreed a "Quiet Hour" during that period each morning, an hour that was formerly full of bustle and activity.

The 75 office employees work in total silence; there is no employee chitchat; outgoing calls are *verboten* and interoffice bells are silent; incoming calls are shut off. Employees use the time to organize themselves and their work for the day. The results have been phenomenal—increased productivity, office efficiency and improved morale. One wonders if a Christian would also benefit in similar ways in his life if he were to decree a Quiet Hour to be spent with God each morning in prayer and Bible reading!

The Wonderful Message of Jesus Revealed

In John 1:4 we read, "In him was life." Jesus Christ is our life: He gave us our physical life; He gives us our spiritual life. There's no life apart from Him; only God can create life; only God can give the abundant life. Some scientists worked long and hard and finally created an egg. It looked like an egg; it tasted like an egg. It contained the food elements of an egg. But it would not hatch a baby chick. Life is a gift from God. In John 1:3 we read that Christ is the Creator of all life.

Jesus Christ is God; He came to earth to dwell with us and to become our Savior so that we might dwell forever with Him!

In John 1:14 we discover that Jesus Christ was made flesh. The Son of God became a man and dwelt among us. He did not cease to be God, but He did become a man. Jesus Christ became a little baby in Bethlehem. He grew as children grow and walked the earth as a man. Verse 14 says that he "dwelt among us;" that means literally that "He pitched his tent in human flesh."

What a wonderful message John reveals to begin his book. It seems only natural to assume that everyone would be interested in such a message: Jesus Christ is God; He came to earth to dwell with us and to become our Savior so that we might dwell forever with Him!

Yet everyone is not waiting to hear the message. John 1:5 tells us that Jesus Christ was a light shining in the darkness, yet the darkness did not comprehend. The Lord Jesus Christ came from heaven to light up this dark world of sin, but many were not willing to take the time to comprehend and understand His message. People are still unwilling to take the time to understand this message.

Perhaps this all sounds exaggerated, but think for a minute about yourself. Have you come to Him and asked Him to be your Savior? (John 3:16-17; Revelation 3:20) "I have written this to you who believe in the Son of God so that you may know you have eternal life" (1 John 5:13). Do you love and serve the Lord Jesus Christ because you really want to? Would you like to do these things?

God said once to Major Ian Thomas, "Seven years with utmost sincerity you have been trying to live for me and on my behalf the life I have been waiting all the time to live through you." "Christ in you, the hope of glory" (Colossians 1:27). Only as we yield ourselves to the Lord Jesus Christ, who dwells within the Christian in the person of the Holy Spirit, can God use our lives abundantly and give to us an abundant life! (1 Corinthians 3:16; 1 Corinthians 6:19; 1 Corinthians 2:10; Romans 5:5).

In John 1:11 we read that the Lord Jesus Christ came unto His own, and His own received Him not. The Lord Jesus Christ was born of the Jewish race and in their land, yet the leaders officially rejected Him as their king and Lord. John 1:12 tells us that as many as received Him, to them gave He power to become sons of God. We are adopted into God's family through faith in the Lord Jesus Christ.

How can you believe on the name of the Lord Jesus Christ? If we take His name apart we will have the answer. Believe that He is Lord; that He is the One with supreme authority. He is Jesus, our Savior. He is Christ, the One sent from heaven. To be a Christian, we believe that Jesus is our Savior, that He is God, and that He is the Lord of our lives. We are told in Revelation 3:20 that we should ask Him to come into our hearts, to be our Savior.

John 1:13 tells us that we are not born by any human effort into God's family: "Not of blood, nor of the will of the flesh, nor of the will of man, but of God." It is God who gives us the right and power to become His children. When we believe and receive Jesus Christ we are a child of God. You are His child because He says so. You may not feel any different, but God says you are different when you receive His Son.

A definition of "a family" was given recently in a P.T.A. magazine. Children were asked to write brief statements on what the family meant to them. One child pictured himself on the floor while his parents reclined on the sofa. Underneath the picture he wrote, "A family is two people in love with children." We can compare this to the Christian family and visualize ourselves reclining at the feet of the Lord Jesus Christ. We have a loving Father in heaven who is Almighty. Trust in His Son, and you will experience His love as a member of His family.

Meeting John the Baptist

We meet John the Baptist in this portion of Scripture beginning with John 1:6. The other three Gospels always refer to him by the name of John the Baptist, but the writer John simply refers to him as "John" (Matthew 3:1-4; Luke 3:2). John's message was one of repentance and reform (Luke 3:10-14). He came to be a witness of "the Light," the Lord Jesus Christ, so that all men might believe in Jesus through John's witness (John 1:7-8). The Lord Jesus said of Himself, "I am the light of the world: he that followeth me shall not walk in darkness, but shall have the light of life" (John 8:12). (John 1:4; John 3:19; John 12:35-37; John 12:46.)

28

John the Baptist declared that he bore witness to Jesus Christ. John said Jesus was to be preferred above him (John 1:15). From Jesus Christ we receive grace, and truth (John 14:6). God's grace means undeserved kindness and love. This does not mean that God has overlooked sin. When the Lord Jesus Christ died on the cross, He bore God's judgment for man's sins. God gives us undeserved forgiveness through His only Son's sacrifice on the cross.

John told the crowd that the law was given by Moses, but grace and truth came by Jesus Christ (John 1:17). The law of Moses was given by God to Moses for the Jewish people to observe. It demanded that the breaking of its law should be punished. It could never be kept perfectly by any man (Galatians 3:11,19,23-24). God provided in Christ undeserved kindness and forgiveness by giving grace and truth through Him.

This portion ends with John the Baptist describing to the crowd that the Lord Jesus Christ declared to them God, whom no man had ever seen. In John 1:18 he describes the "only begotten Son, which is in the bosom of the Father." What a precious resting place this (He) is. Every person who comes to the Lord Jesus Christ in faith has this peace and love and rest from God the Father. Each person is adopted into God's family through faith in His only begotten Son (Romans 8:15-17; Titus 3:7; Ephesians 3:17-21).

The Lord Jesus Christ—The Lamb of God
John 1:19-34

When John knew for sure who Jesus was (John 1:19-23) he was ready to do the important work that God had given him. John told the priests and Levites, "There standeth one among you, whom ye know not; He it is, who coming after me is preferred before me, whose shoe's latchet I am not worthy to unloose" (John 1:26-27). The day after the priests and Levites had questioned him, John introduced Jesus Christ. The event took place in the region of the Jordan River where John was baptizing people for repentance of sin (Luke 3:3). John saw the Lord Jesus and said to the crowd, "Behold the Lamb of God, which taketh away the sin of the world" (John 1:29).

The reason John called Jesus the Lamb of God was to show that He was the final sacrifice for sin. In the Old Testament we read in Exodus 12:3 "Speak ye unto all the congregation of Israel, saying, In the tenth day of this month they shall take to them every man a lamb, according to the house of their fathers, a lamb for an house." This was the institution of the Passover sacrifice of the lamb in order that the Israelites' children would be spared the plague which would pass over

Egypt as a form of God's judgment upon their sin. This plague would kill all of the firstborn sons in the households.

God protected the Israelites by means of this passover lamb. A lamb was one of the animals used for a sacrifice in the Old Testament. "If he offer a lamb for his offering, then he shall offer it before the Lord. And he shall lay his hand upon the head of his offering, and kill it before the tabernacle" (Leviticus 3:7-8). Since the Lord Jesus Christ came to die for us to make Himself a sacrifice for our sins, He is called the "Lamb of God." He was sacrificed for us. He died to remove the guilt of sin from everyone who comes to Him and asks for forgiveness. As the lamb in the Old Testament shed its blood in the sacrifices, so the lamb of God shed His blood on the cross. "Without shedding of blood is no remission [of sin]" (Hebrews 9:22).

John went on to describe what had happened at the baptism of Jesus. The last phrase of John 1:33 tells us that Jesus will give the Holy Spirit to His followers. The Lord forgives our sins when we come to Him and receive Him as our Savior. He also gives us the Holy Spirit so that we have new life and new power to live for Him.

The most important discovery that you could ever help someone to find is the Lord Jesus Christ as Savior! The famous physician Sir James Simpson was the first to employ ether in obstetrics and to discover the important qualities and proper use of chloroform. A group of young scientists who highly respected Dr. Simpson asked him, "What do you count as the most outstanding discovery you have ever made?"

With tears welling up in his eyes he lifted up his head and said, "Young men, the greatest discovery I have ever made is that Jesus Christ is my Savior; that is by far the most important thing a person can ever come to know!"

Yes, this is the greatest discovery you can make. Whenever anyone discovers Christ, Jesus Christ Himself makes good His promises by the transforming power of His Holy Spirit who lives in the Christian (John 14:16-17; John 16:7-14; 1 Corinthians 2:4). Are you claiming this power of the Holy Spirit?

Those Who Followed in Faith
John 1:35-51

Another day passed and John the Baptist was talking with two of his disciples. One of these disciples was Andrew (John 1:40). The other disciple is thought to have been the apostle John. Jesus was again identified as the Lamb of God. When Andrew met Christ he wanted his brother to know Him, too. Andrew and Peter were from

Bethsaida. Andrew found Simon and told him, "We have found the Messiah" (John 1:41).

Next we meet another disciple of Jesus, Philip, in John 1:43-44. Philip came from the same city as Andrew and Peter. But neither Andrew nor Peter told him about Christ. Perhaps Philip did not seem important enough to find. The Lord Himself found Philip and said to him, "Follow me." Perhaps Philip did not seem important to men, but the Lord considered him important. He called him to be one of His disciples. In John 1:45 Philip found Nathanael, and introduced him to Jesus.

Nathanael was from the town of Cana (John 21:2). He was skeptical of anyone who came from Nazareth. It was such a little, unimportant place that Nathanael said with derision, "Can there any good thing come out of Nazareth?" (John 1:46). He was not so skeptical that he would not accept Philip's invitation so he came to see for himself. The Lord Jesus paid Nathanael a compliment. "Behold an Israelite indeed, in whom is no guile!" (John 1:47). Nathanael was an honest forthright man according to the Lord Jesus' statement.

In the last verse of the first chapter the Lord calls Himself the "Son of man." There is an interesting point about the use of this title. Only the Lord Himself used it to describe Himself. The title did not tell of the glory or power of Jesus Christ. This was a title which told of His humility. Perhaps this is one reason that His friends did not use it.

Yes, Andrew, Philip, John and Nathanael all "found Christ." For them it meant poverty, hardship, suffering, persecution, and in fact, death by execution for most. Yet they also discovered in Him a Savior, Lord, Companion and Friend. Those who come to the Lord today find Him equally precious.

Study Questions

Before you begin your study this week:

1. Pray each day and ask God to speak to you through His Holy Spirit.
2. Use only your Bible to answer the following questions.
3. Write down your answers and, where called for, include the verses you used.
4. Challenge questions are for those who have the time and who wish to do them.
5. Personal questions are to be shared with your study group only if you wish to share.
6. As you study, look for a verse to memorize this week. Write it down, carry it with you, tack it to your bulletin board, tape it to the dashboard of your car. Make a real effort to learn this verse and its reference.

FIRST DAY: Read all of the preceding notes and look up all of the Scriptures given.

1. What was a helpful or new thought from the overview of John 1?

2. What personal application did you select to apply to your own life?

SECOND DAY: Read all of John 2 concentrating on verses 1-11.

1. Who attended the marriage in Cana of Galilee? Give verses with the names.

2. What did Mary say to the servants at the wedding concerning the Lord Jesus? Give verse.

3. What did the servants do in obedience to the Lord Jesus' instructions?

4. What was the miracle which the Lord Jesus did at the wedding feast?

5. What were some results of this miracle? Give verse.

6. **Challenge:** John 2:5 contains the interesting words "Whatsoever he saith unto you, do it." It is pleasing to God when the Christian is obedient to Jesus Christ. The following verses speak of this loving obedience. Put them into your own words, using your name to personalize the statement, if you wish to.

   1 Samuel 12:24

   Ephesians 6:6

THIRD DAY: Read John 2:12-13 with Exodus 12.

1. Where did the Lord Jesus go after the wedding and who went with Him? Try to find this place on the Bible map.

2. After a few days passed by, where did the Lord Jesus go next? Why did He go there?

3. From what was the original Passover lamb's blood to protect God's people? Give verse from Exodus, chapter 12.

4. What did Exodus 12:14 and Exodus 12:24-25 instruct the Jewish people to do?

5. **Challenge:** How did God deliver the Jewish people from slavery in Egypt as a result of the plague which He sent to all homes where the Passover was not observed? See Exodus 12:27-34. Summarize your answer in a short statement if possible.

6 a. What does 1 Corinthians 5:7 say about Jesus Christ and the Passover?

   b. (Personal) What does 1 Corinthians 5:7 mean to you? Share if possible with your discussion group.

34

FOURTH AND FIFTH DAY: Read John 2:14-17.

1. When the Lord Jesus arrived in Jerusalem what did He find at the Temple? Give verse from John.

2. What was the Lord Jesus' response to what He found going on in the Temple grounds?

3. What name did the Lord Jesus give to God in this passage?

4. Psalm 69 is a psalm which is prophetically speaking of the Lord Jesus Christ. Find the verse that the disciples remember in John 2:17 and state where it is found in this psalm.

5. **Challenge:** Read through the entire Psalm 69 and choose your favorite verses which emphasize:

   Christ's suffering for you

Christ's love for you

Prayer to Christ for His help

Giving praise to God

6. (Personal) Which of the verses in Psalm 69 meant the most to you? Write down the verse and give the reason why you chose it. Share if possible with your discussion group.

SIXTH DAY: Read John 2:18-25.

1. What did the religious leaders ask of the Lord Jesus Christ which would supposedly show His authority and right to cleanse the Temple?

2 a. What was the Lord Jesus Christ's reply to these Jewish religious leaders, and what was their reaction to His reply?

ᴅ. What temple was the Lord Jesus really referring to?

36

3. How does 1 Corinthians 6:19 describe the body of a Christian?

4 a. **Challenge:** How would 1 Corinthians 6:20 help you to understand the Lord Jesus' words "Destroy this temple, and in three days I will raise it up" in John 2:19?

   b. (Personal) What challenge for your own life do you find in 1 Corinthians 6:19-20?

5 a. How does 1 Peter 1:18-19 explain why Christ's "temple" was destroyed, and how is Jesus Christ referred to in these verses?

   b. (Personal) Do you know who has redeemed you from sin (Romans 3:23) after reading 1 Peter 1:18-19? If you know and have received the Lord Jesus Christ as your Redeemer, how are you sharing this Good News with others?

6 a. When did the disciples of Jesus remember what He had said in Jerusalem after He had cleansed the Temple? What did they believe after they remembered His words? See John 2:18-22. Give verse please.

b. Which verse meant the most to you this week? Did you choose to memorize it?

THE BEGINNING OF HIS SIGNS
John 2

Study Notes

The Wedding Feast at Cana John 2:1-12

John selected certain miracles out of many, to teach us what God wishes us to receive for our own lives. In the original Greek, the word "miracle" could be translated "sign." The Lord Jesus began to work miracles in Cana, a quiet village near Nazareth, located in an obscure corner of Galilee. Jesus' first miracle occurred on the third day after He arrived in Galilee (John 2:1). The occasion was a wedding, attended by Jesus, His mother and His disciples (John 2:2). It was a happy event, which Jesus gladly shared.

A wedding in Palestine took place late in the evening, after a feast. After the ceremony the married couple was conducted to their home by the wedding guests. It must have been very picturesque as the guests carried flaming torches and escorted the couple under a canopy to their home. This was a long procession for they wanted as many people as possible to have an opportunity to give their good wishes to the couple as they walked to their new home.

The married couple did not go away for a honeymoon, but stayed in their home and had open house for one week for all of their friends. They wore crowns and dressed in their bridal clothes each day. In fact, they were dressed as king and queen and their word was law for this week. There was much poverty and hard work among people in general, so this special week was set aside to be completely joyous for the bridal couple and all of their friends. There was much feasting and fellowship during this time.

39

Society's Problem with Alcoholism

It was traditional at a wedding feast to serve wine, although drunkenness was a great disgrace. Wine was used in Old and New Testament days, but dedicated persons such as priests were commanded to abstain from using it. Today, alcoholism presents a problem to society for many reasons, among them that alcoholic drinks can be obtained cheaply and people too often have a low value of human life and dignity.

Our nation has taken great interest in most of the ills that threaten human life, yet there is indifference toward the proven killer, alcohol. If a product is shown to contain an ingredient which appears to produce cancer in mice, it is immediately forced off the market by governmental action. Yet approximately nine million Americans are excessive drinkers and there seems to be little concern over this. At least half of the automobile deaths per year are directly traced to drinking. An alcoholic's life span is shortened by at least 10 years. Over three-fourths of all prison inmates have been sentenced for crimes they committed after drinking alcohol. Today, many teenagers have turned from drugs to alcohol for their "high" because it is so much more easily obtainable and acceptable in our society. Recently a group of doctors at the University of Washington discovered a consistent pattern of serious birth defects and infant mortality among children born to alcoholic mothers. Yet when all of these sad statistics are cited, most people simply do not seem concerned.

We must be concerned when the National Council on Alcoholism reports that one out of every 14 employed persons in America is an alcoholic, and that they cost American business 4.3 billion dollars a year in absenteeism, sloppy work and eventual training of replacements. The National Institute on Alcohol Abuse and Alcoholism estimates that the total dollar cost of alcoholism may be as high as $15 billion a year. In most cases, by the time it is recognized that drinking is leading to trouble, the drinker is hooked.

Scripture teaches that any practice that abuses the human body of a Christian, described as the temple of the Holy Spirit is wrong (1 Corinthians 6:20). Paul made this statement, "All things are lawful unto me, but all things are not expedient" (1 Corinthians 6:12). *The Living Bible* paraphrases Paul's quote in 1 Corinthians 6:11-12 as follows: "There was a time when some of you were just like that but now your sins are washed away, and you are set apart for God, and he has accepted you because of what the Lord Jesus Christ and the Spirit of our God have done for you. I can do anything I want to if Christ has not said no, but some of these things aren't good for me. Even if I am allowed to do them, I'll refuse to if I think that they might get such a grip on me that I can't easily stop when I want to."

The Christian needs to remember to stop short of anything that brings offense (Matthew 18:6), or that may cause another person to stumble. "The right thing to do is to quit eating meat or drinking wine or doing anything else that offends your brother or makes him sin" (Romans 14:21). Any Christian who takes leadership in the church needs to remember God's words in 1 Timothy 3:3, "He must not be a drinker or quarrelsome, but he must be gentle and kind." The mother of John Wesley wrote: "Whatever weakens your reason, impairs the tenderness of your conscience, obscures your sense of God, or takes off the relish of spiritual things, in short, whatever increases the strength and authority of your body over your mind, that thing is sin to you, however innocent it may be in itself."

We all need to examine ourselves as we think of the environmental abuse of alcohol in our society. The drinking of wine is not specifically condemned in the Scriptures except when drunkenness is involved. Therefore, the Christian must not condemn other Christians who drink wine without drunkenness. However, each Christian needs to pray and ask God for His perfect will concerning this issue. Remember that the Lord Jesus wants your body—from the head to the foot! "And so, dear brothers, I plead with you to give your bodies to God. Let them be a living sacrifice, holy—the kind he can accept. When you think of what he has done for you, is this too much to ask? Don't copy the behavior and customs of this world, but be a new and different person with a fresh newness in all you do and think. Then you will learn from your own experience how his ways will really satisfy you" (Romans 12:1-2).

Alcoholism is a major evil which demands some action on the part of society. A Christian should be concerned with the well-being of society and therefore has an obligation to take part in the battle against this evil which is destroying it. The problem of alcoholism demands drastic measures, which may even call for sacrifice of personal freedom in Christ, to help people around us with this major problem. Will you ask God to show you His will concerning this matter? God always supplies the power for all that He requires of us (Zechariah 4:6)!

Mary Sets an Example for Us

Mary saw that there was a crisis at the wedding (John 2:3). The Coptic Gospels of Egypt suggest that Mary was a sister of the bridegroom's mother. Other writings suggest that John himself was the bridegroom since his mother was Salome, Mary's sister. We are not certain that these extra details are true, but perhaps this is the reason that Mary took such an active part in this wedding feast. She was concerned about the lack of refreshments and the guests still waiting to be served. She went immediately to Jesus and told Him what had happened. Hospitality in this area was a sacred duty, and it would be a shame for the bride and bridegroom to lack refreshments for their guests.

The Lord Jesus said, "Woman, what have I to do with thee?" (John 2:4). "Woman" is a term of tenderness and is the same word that Jesus used when on the cross He provided for Mary to be cared for by John (John 19:26). In *Homer*, the word "Woman" is a title by which Odysseus addressed Penelope, his beloved wife. In English, we might better translate the word "Lady."

Mary was confident in the Lord Jesus Christ. Undoubtedly she had often gone to Him with her own problems and seen Him work out the very best solution for them. This is the blessed example set by Mary, the mother of our Savior. Although she couldn't understand some things Jesus said and did, she trusted Him fully, knowing He never made a mistake. She therefore instructed the servants at the wedding, who were in need of wine, to obey His every command (John 2:5). Her faith was rewarded, for Jesus performed the miracle necessary to supply that which was lacking. Mary's faith can be the example for us. Allow Jesus Christ to control and aid you in handling the affairs of your life. Whatever your needs are in your home, personal relationships, business relationships, or any other area of need in your life—the Lord Jesus will meet them if you will respond with the heart attitude that Mary expressed in John 2:5, "Whatsoever he saith unto you, do it." Remember that God does not demand of you success, or profit—just loving obedience!

> "Whatever God asks you to do, do it,
> Fill the vessels to the brim;
> But always remember it's His battle
> So leave the miracle to Him."

"For the battle is not your's, but God's" (2 Chronicles 20:15).

Mary turned to Jesus when things went wrong. An old legend tells us that those who lived in Nazareth who felt weary and upset, would go and look at Jesus, and somehow all their troubles rolled away. It is still true that anyone who knows Jesus Christ well will instinctively turn to Him when things go wrong. He is always there to help. Even when it seemed that Jesus refused Mary's request, she still believed that He would solve the problem at the wedding feast. She had the kind of faith which could trust even when it did not understand. She could say to the servants, "Whatsoever he saith unto you, do it."

In all of our lives comes times of deep distress when we do not understand why things are as they are. We cannot understand the meaning of everything that happens. Yet believers in Christ can have the same hope that Mary had! We can trust the Lord to work out our problem even though we don't understand how He will handle it. Are you willing to trust the Lord Jesus Christ with your problem today?

> *We realize that Jesus knew He had come into this world for the purpose of giving Himself on the cross for our sins. He came to do the will of God.*

In John 2:4 Jesus was saying, "I know what you want. You want me to reveal who I am to the world. My work is not to perform signs. My work is to die. It is not time for that now. My hour is not yet come."

All throughout Jesus' life He talked about His hour. In John 7:6,8 it is the hour that He reveals Himself as the Messiah. In John 12:23 and John 17:1 (Matthew 26:18,45; Mark 14:41) it is the hour of His crucifixion and His death.

We realize that Jesus knew He had come into this world for the purpose of giving Himself on the cross for our sins. He came to do the will of God (Luke 12:47, 22:42; John 6:38). The Lord Jesus Christ came into this world to fulfill the purpose of God in redeeming man from sin (John 3:16; Romans 6:23). We, too, should not think of our own wishes and desires, but ask God what His purpose is for us in His world.

The Lord Jesus came not to do the will of His mother, but to please His Father in heaven. As He said, "I seek not mine own will, but the will of the Father which hath sent me" (John 5:30). We cannot order God around; we are to listen for His orders to us! Someone has written most beautifully:

"In Galilee, in days of yore, when some were conscious of a need,
The mother of our Lord arose and gave them counsel—wise indeed!
She did not try to order things. Ah no! She knew the better way;
So she directed them to Him who could supply the need that day.
Her message through the years rolls on, still bringing counsel wise
    and true:
That whatsoever Christ may say, we quickly should obey—and do!
For He's the One to order things, He is the answer to our need;

43

He saves and keeps and satisfies, and if we let Him, He will lead.
And so we still may sweetly guide lost sinners to our loving Lord;
Then wondrous service, joy divine—to teach them to obey His
    Word!"
(See John 2:5.)

The Lord Jesus turned from His mother and spoke to the servants
who were at work nearby (John 2:6-10). The command the Lord
Jesus gave was simple and direct, and the response of the servants
was immediate. Jesus said, "Fill the waterpots with water" and the
servants filled them to the brim.

Next Jesus commanded, "Draw out now and bear it unto the gov-
ernor of the feast."

It is not surprising that the result was the best wine. Imagine how
the servants felt! Imagine what Mary thought! Each of them must
have looked in real astonishment at the miracle so quickly and quietly
performed. The servants' obedience gave them a share in the first
miracle that Christ did.

John records that this was the beginning of Jesus' miracles (John
2:11). John chose certain signs to show Jesus as the Christ, the Son
of God. This is the first of those signs (John 20:30-31). John said of
this first sign, "This miracle at Cana in Galilee was Jesus' first public
demonstration of his heaven-sent power" (John 2:11). The result was
that the disciples believed in Him.

Do you suppose that the servants did, too? The Bible does not
give the answer. As you have read what the Lord Jesus has done, will
you follow Him and believe in Him wherever He leads you? The disciples followed Jesus from Cana to Capernaum along with His mother
and His brothers (John 2:12).

The First Temple Purification by the Lord Jesus John 2:13-25

When the time of the Jewish Passover was near, Jesus went to Jerusalem. The first Passover was the feast eaten just before the Israelites left Egypt. Every year the Jews obeyed the command of God and
recalled their escape from slavery by observing this special feast. The
Passover was one of the three important feasts of the Jews. It was
the time of celebrating their deliverance from Egypt (Exodus 23:14).

The Lord went to the Temple on Mount Moriah in Jerusalem.
This was the place where Abraham offered Isaac (Genesis 22:2), and
here David purchased the threshing floor of Ornan and offered sacrifices to the Lord when the plague was stopped (1 Chronicles 21:21-
28; 2 Chronicles 3:1). The Temple area had three courts. The outer

44

court was called the "court of Gentiles." Next was the "court of Women." The innermost court was for the Israelite men only. The Temple building was in this court.

When the Lord Jesus entered into the court of Gentiles He found it filled with animals and birds to be used for sacrifices. It was easier for the Jews to buy the animals at the Temple than to transport them from their homes. Instead of the Temple being a quiet and worshipful place, it smelled and sounded like a circus. Orientals are great traders, and every transaction ends with tremendous confusion and noise. In addition to the animals, money changers had set up their tables. These men were bankers who, for a sixth discount, changed foreign coins into shekels in order that people might pay their Temple tax. Picture such a scene in the outer court of the place where men came to worship God.

The action of the Lord was dramatic. He took some of the cords that had been used to tie the animals and made a whip or scourge of them. "He drove them all out of the temple, and the sheep, and the oxen; and poured out the changers' money, and overthrew the tables" (John 2:15). If Jesus' actions were astonishing, His words must have caused even greater amazement. "Get these things out of here. Don't turn my Father's house into a market!" (John 2:16). This is the first time in John's Gospel that Jesus called God "My Father." The words must have surprised the Jewish men! They were not used to such familiarity with God.

The people wanted proof of Jesus' authority (John 2:18). The answer that Jesus gave was another surprise. "Destroy this temple, and in three days I will raise it up" (John 2:19). The only sign that Jesus spoke about was that of His death and resurrection. This is the first time He spoke of His sacrifice and resurrection. When Jesus Christ was asked to prove His authority, He gave the sign of His resurrection (Matthew 12:38-40). The resurrection of Christ is the supreme sign of His deity. The Jews did not understand the words of the Lord. They looked at the Temple building and reminded Jesus that the Temple had already taken 46 years to build and that it was not finished yet (John 2:20)! In fact, work on the Temple was continued until A.D. 64 just six years before it was destroyed by a Roman attack led by Titus.

John tells us that after the resurrection of the Lord Jesus, the disciples remembered these words which the Lord had spoken, and believed him (John 2:22). Some of the people in Jerusalem believed in Him also as a result of the miracles which He performed (John 2:22-23). Some people believed, others did not.

A classic cartoon shows a little English school boy standing outside a candy store. The window is filled with jars and boxes of candy.

But there on the window is a poster which says, "Do not lick the window." We smile, but we may be smiling at ourselves. Are there not many who are standing outside the storehouse of God's provision through Jesus Christ for forgiveness of sins, looking in wistfully, and wondering how on earth they can make this good gift of forgiveness theirs. We do not have to stand outside the window! God invites us to Himself! "Look! I have been standing at the door and I am constantly knocking. If anyone hears me calling him and opens the door, I will come in and fellowship with him and he with me" (Revelation 3:20). The Lord Jesus Christ is waiting for us to invite Him into our lives to be our Savior and Lord. If you are a Christian are you standing outside the storehouse of God's provision for your daily life? God invites you to help yourself to all the things necessary for a life of joy. Don't stand outside any longer. Come on in for this, too! "I am come that they might have life, and that they might have it more abundantly" (John 10:10). Faith is a *F*antastic *A*dventure *I*n *T*rusting *H*im.

> It is not try, but trust.
> It is not do, but done.
> Our God has planned for us
> Great victory through His Son!

"Loving God means doing what he tells us to do, and really, that isn't hard at all; for every child of God can obey him, defeating sin and evil pleasure by trusting Christ to help him" (see 1 John 5:3-4). Will you pray for wisdom, for help—for anything that will be used for God's glory? (1 John 5:14-15). The Lord Jesus loves to be asked. On several occasions He rebuked men for having too little faith, but He never rebuked for asking too much!

> **The Lord who made you, redeemed you with His blood, has the right and the power to do a work in your life, if you will only ask Him.**

The Bible teaches that when we are Christians, our bodies are the temple of the Holy Spirit. (See 1 Corinthians 6:19-20.) Since this is true, we should consider whether we need to be cleansed. Are we a fit place for God to dwell in? Do we worship God in all that we do? If you want the Lord to cleanse your life and make it a fit "temple," you will have to let the Lord have complete control.

God cannot really cleanse your life if you will not let Him into every room. Will you give Him the key to all of your life? May He have the library where you read? know and approve of the books you read? come into the recreation room where you relax? be a part of your social times? come into the living room where you sit with your family? enter your private room where you go when you want to be alone? Are you ashamed when you realize that Christ watches and hears the way you talk and treat your family? Is there any reason that you do not want Him to have control of your most innermost secrets? All of this He must have if He is to make your life really a "temple in which He can dwell."

The Lord who made you, redeemed you with His blood, has the right and the power to do a work in your life, if you will only ask Him. Jesus Christ is still the miracle worker. Are you willing now to ask the Lord Jesus Christ to work out all of this in your life? Why not stop right now and talk to the Lord Jesus and ask Him for His help in your life today?

Study Questions

Before you begin your study this week:
1. Pray each day and ask God to speak to you through His Holy Spirit.
2. Use only your Bible to answer the following questions.
3. Write down your answers, and, where called for, include the verses you used.
4. Challenge questions are for those who have the time and who wish to do them.
5. Personal questions are to be shared with your study group only if you wish to share.
6. As you study, look for a verse to memorize this week. Write it down, carry it with you, tack it to your bulletin board, tape it to the dashboard of your car. Make a real effort to learn the verse and its reference.

FIRST DAY: Read all of the preceding notes and look up all of the Scriptures given.

1. What was a helpful or new thought from the overview of John 2?

2. What personal application did you select to apply to your own life this week?

SECOND DAY: Read all of John 3 concentrating on verses 1-6.

1. Who was Nicodemus?

2. What time did he choose to go and question the Lord Jesus?

3. How did Nicodemus compliment Jesus Christ in John 3:2?

4. How did the Lord Jesus tell Nicodemus that he needed to have a second birthday to enter the kingdom of God?

5. Did Nicodemus misunderstand the meaning of Jesus Christ's words in John 3:3? Give the reason for your answer.

6 a. **Challenge:** How can a person be "born again" as Jesus stated you must be to enter God's kingdom? See John 1:12-13.

b. In which verse in this passage does Jesus describe two ways a person is born?

c. (Personal) Have you had two birthdays, both the physical and spiritual?

d. (Personal) How would you describe being "born again" to a friend?

THIRD DAY: Read John 3:7-11.

1. How does Jesus reemphasize the importance of a second birthday in John 3:7? What word does He use which makes it essential for every person to have a spiritual birth?

2. How does John 14:6 emphasize the fact that there is only one way to be "born again" into God's family?

3. According to John 3:9-10 do you believe Nicodemus understood Jesus and was "born of the Spirit" at this time?

4. Is it possible to be a "master" of knowledge today and yet not comprehend spiritual truths? Do you believe there are many modern day "Nicodemus people"?

5. Which verse in this passage indicates that Nicodemus was unwilling to receive the truth the Lord Jesus was telling him?

6 a. Challenge: The idea of being "born again" is found throughout all of the New Testament writings. What do the following verses say about a "new birth"? You may put them into your own words and personalize them by putting your name into each verse if you wish to.

   1 Peter 1:23

   James 1:18

   b. (Personal) Has 2 Corinthians 5:17 become a personal experience in your life? What old things have passed away? What has become new to you? Share with your discussion group if possible.

FOURTH DAY: Read John 3:12-21.

1. **Challenge:** Read Numbers 21:9 and remember that the serpent symbolizes Satan in the Bible (see Genesis 3:1-5 and Revelation 20:1-3). This serpent lifted up on a pole was a type of judgment on sin, so that when the Israelites looked up at this "judgment for their sin" they were saved and did not die. What do you believe the Son of man (Jesus Christ—Perfect God—Perfect Man) had to be "lifted up" on as judgment for man's sins?

2. What are the joyous results of looking up to the Lord Jesus Christ with faith in our hearts that He will forgive us our sins? See John 3:14-18.

3. Is there any person so good that he does not need to "look up to" Jesus Christ for forgiveness of sins? What do Romans 3:23 and Romans 6:23 say about this?

   Romans 3:23

   Romans 6:23

4. Romans 6:23 speaks of a "gift" from God. What does Ephesians 2:8-9 say about this gift of God?

5 a. What does Ephesians 2:8-9 mean to you?

b. (Personal) Have you ever been in the position of trying to work your way into God's favor by doing "good things" called works? Do you now realize that it is only your faith in Jesus Christ that makes you acceptable to God?

6. Read John 3:21 remembering that "the light" is the Lord Jesus Christ. What does John 8:12 say about the light?

FIFTH DAY: Read John 3:21 with Ephesians 4:19-32.

John 3:21 speaks of responding to Christ's light. Read Ephesians 4:19-32 and put down in the space given what the Christian is to "put away" or cast aside. Then write down the things listed in this passage that the Christian is to "be" when he is walking in Christ's light by faith.

1. The Christian is to cast aside:

2. The Christian is to "be":

3. As you have listed these things "to be" and "not to be" as a Christian, it would seem humanly impossible to fully please God in these ways. Yet, He has given us a mighty Person of power to empower our lives and make them what they should be as Christians. Who is this Person of power God gives to the Christian? Read Romans 5:5 and 2 Timothy 1:7,14.

4. (Personal) After reading Ephesians 4:19-32 which part of this passage touched your heart the most? Would you like to yield yourself right now to the Holy Spirit's power to give you a victory in your life? Why not pray about it now? Write down the victory you are claiming in your life by the power of the Holy Spirit. Put the date and time down in your Bible and begin to trust God from this moment on for His victory in your life!

5. and 6. How does Titus 3:5-6 speak of God's gift of the Holy Ghost to the Christian?

SIXTH DAY: Read John 3:22-36.

1. How does John the Baptist describe himself in this passage? Give verses.

2 a. What does John the Baptist say in John 3:27 which every Christian needs to remember?

b. Challenge: If Christians remember this truth do you think there would be pride, controversy and envy among God's children?

3 a. Envy, greed, bitterness and pride would fall away if each Christian were willing to say what John the Baptist did in John 3:30. What did he say?

b. (Personal) Will you choose to repeat this statement as a prayer right now and trust the Lord to work it out each day, moment by moment this week?

4. How does Galatians 2:20 add to the thoughts in John 3:30? If possible, put this verse into your own words and put your own name in the verse where "I" is used to make it personal.

5. How are the thoughts of the first part of John 3 summarized in John 3:35-36?

6 a. (Personal) Christ's coming makes man responsible to either choose to be born again by faith in His forgiveness and love, or to choose God's condemnation of eternal separation from Him. *"For God so loved* the world, that he gave his only begotten Son, that whosoever believeth in him should not perish, but have everlasting life."* Have you chosen to receive His Son by faith?

b. Are you willing to share Jesus Christ with others? How are you doing this sharing this week?

"YOU MUST BE BORN AGAIN"

John 3

Study Notes

Jesus Talks with Nicodemus John 3:1-21

When something unusual takes place it does not take long for the news to spread. In the spring of A.D. 27, the city of Jerusalem was buzzing with the report of several unusual events. One was the story of a man who had entered the city and disturbed the whole way of life of the people. The Temple area had been cleared of the sacrificial animals and the money changers. Other works which this same man had done were being talked about. He was unusual. He was definitely news! Finally, the rulers of the Jews became curious about who He was. One of these Jewish teachers wanted to see for himself, and so Nicodemus came to visit Jesus Christ.

John 3:1 teaches us three facts of truth about Nicodemus. First, we learn that he was a Pharisee, a member of a strict religious sect among the Jews. They put special emphasis on the exact and literal observance of the law. Not only did they follow the law literally, but they began to extract from the great principles of the law a great number of rules and regulations to govern many situations in life. They changed the law of the great principles into the legalism of bylaws and regulations.

The best example of what they did is seen in the Sabbath law. God had directed in the Bible to keep the Sabbath holy and that on that day no work was to be done either by man, servants or animals. In later centuries, rabbis and scribes spent hour after hour and generation upon generation defining "work," and listing the things that could or could not be done on the Sabbath. The rules they developed finally extended to 24 chapters in the Mishnah.

The Talmud is the explanatory commentary on the Mishnah, and in the Jerusalem Talmud the section explaining the Sabbath law is 64 and a half columns long. What all of these rules did was to say things such as, "To tie a knot on the Sabbath is to work." But a knot had to be defined! Some knots made a man guilty of work such as the knot of camel drivers and sailors. On the other hand some knots could be tied quite legally. A woman could tie the strings of her cap and those of her girdle, the straps of shoes or sandals, and a knot to secure the skins that served as containers for wine and oil!

The situation could become quite humorous. A man could not tie a rope on a barrel to draw water on the Sabbath unless he was clever enough to think of tying the barrel to a woman's girdle and letting it down into the well! For a knot in a girdle was quite legal! The Jewish people themselves thought highly of the Pharisees. The Jews believed the Pharisees to be the most deeply religious men of the day. The scribes worked out all of the regulations and the Pharisees dedicated their lives to keeping them. The name Pharisee means "the Separated Ones." The Pharisees separated themselves from all ordinary life in order to keep every detail of the law of the scribes.

Nicodemus Was an Important Pharisee

The fact that Nicodemus was a Pharisee, who regarded his own goodness and kind of life as pleasing to God, makes it astonishing that he would wish to talk to Jesus at all! The second and third facts we learn about Nicodemus are that he was a ruler of the Jews and this meant that he was a member of the Sanhedrin, the supreme Jewish court of justice. This court was the final authority on the interpretation of the Mosaic Law. Thus we know that Nicodemus was an important man in Jerusalem. John is the only Gospel in which the name Nicodemus appears. John tells us of this meeting in John 3. He tells of an occasion when Nicodemus was one of the rich men who assisted in the burial of Jesus (John 19:39-42).

This important Pharisee was interested in spiritual matters enough to come to Jesus Christ one night. There could possibly have been two reasons for his coming to the Lord Jesus at night. It may have been a sign of caution as Nicodemus may not have wished his fellow members of the Sanhedrin to know of his visit. We must not condemn or call Nicodemus a coward, for it was better to come at night than not to come at all to Jesus. With all of his prejudices in his upbringing, and his whole view of life from his Pharisaic training, it was a miracle that he had the courage to come at all to Jesus. Another reason Nicodemus chose the night for his visit may have been that rabbis always considered this the best time to study the law, when a man could be undisturbed. We know that Jesus was surrounded by crowds during the day, and Nicodemus may have wanted a private, undisturbed meeting with the Lord Jesus.

He began the conversation with a compliment, "Rabbi, we know that You have come from God as a teacher; for no one can do these signs that You do, unless God is with him" (John 3:2). Nicodemus did well as far as he went. The mistake was that he did not go far enough. Jesus Christ is not just "from God" nor is it just that "God is with him." He is God! Jesus was not a "teacher come from God" such as Moses, Isaiah, and later Paul, the disciples, Luther, Calvin and Augustine. There are many men today who are teachers come from God. However, only once did God come to teach. God came in the flesh, in the person of Jesus Christ as perfect God-perfect Man to teach us.

The Lord Jesus went directly to the heart of Nicodemus's problem, "Truly, truly, I say to you, unless one is born again, he cannot see the kingdom of God" (John 3:3). Nicodemus considered himself a good man. He was one of the religious leaders of his day. But Jesus told him that he was not good enough. Nicodemus had to be born again. In case Nicodemus did not understand that he was included in the general statement of verse three, Jesus said directly, "Ye must be born again" (John 3:7). No one is good enough to get to heaven without Christ's help. It is not enough to do the best you can. It is not enough to do better than your friends. No one can enter heaven and be with God forever unless he has come to Christ and been born again. We read in the book of Job, "How then can man be justified with God? or how can he be clean that is born of a woman? Behold even to the moon, and it shineth not; yea, the stars are not pure in his sight. How much less man, that is a worm?" (Job 25:4-6).

Man Needs a New Heart

The story is told of a missionary who visited the hut of a native and became completely nauseated by the filthy floor on which they had to walk and sit. He suggested that they get some soap and water and scrub the dirty surface. But the native replied, "It would only make it worse. You see, the floor is just clay—packed down and dried. Add water and it turns to mud. The more you try to wash it, the worse the mess becomes." Yes, the hut needed something besides an earthen floor. So it is with the human heart; it is hard and dry and nothing will help it. Man needs a new heart! We must be born from above! While the gift of God is eternal life through Jesus Christ our Lord, to make it yours you must personally receive this wonderful Savior and the redemption He offers. Have you done this? If not, do it now (Romans 5:1,6,8-11).

God's gift of love to the world was His only begotten Son (John 3:16). Yet the giving of this gift does not make it yours. An example of this was illustrated by a doctor who asked a young lad, "Does the giving of a gift make it yours?"

The boy replied, "Well, I suppose you must take it to make it really yours."

"Exactly," said the doctor, "and so Christ must be taken as God's gift. I'm a physician," he went on, "while I'm not your doctor, am I?"

"No," said the boy.

"Why not?" he asked.

"Because we never chose you as our doctor," was the reply.

"That's right! So, too, Christ is the Savior, but he is not your Savior unless you take him."

You have to put in a conversion kit any time you change your energy. This is what happens when we leave human power and start running on divine power. The manufacturer, who happens to be God, is ready to give us a conversion experience kit so we can have His power and His energy.

While the gift of God is eternal life through Jesus Christ our Lord, to make it yours you must personally receive this wonderful Savior and the redemption He offers. Have you done this?

Nicodemus did not understand what Jesus meant by being "born again." He revealed his lack of comprehension by the words in John 3:4, "How can a man be born when he is old? Can he enter a second time into his mother's womb, and be born?" Jesus' reply was, "I say to you, unless one is born of water and the Spirit, he cannot enter into the kingdom of God. That which is born of the flesh is flesh, and that which is born of Spirit is spirit" (John 3:5-6). Jesus Christ is pointing out to Nicodemus that He is speaking of a supernatural birth rather than delivery of a newborn baby from its mother's womb.

In John 3:5, Jesus mentions water to Nicodemus. Matthew Henry, the commentator, and others believe that "water" here refers to baptism, but not in the sense that the *physical* element of water accomplishes the new birth. Rather, they suggest that baptism illustrates or demonstrates *spiritual* change—a new birth.

Still others believe that water refers to the cleansing and renewing power of the Word of God. I lean toward that interpretation myself. For, as Scripture says, "How can a young man stay pure? By reading your word and following its rules" (Psalm 119:9; see Psalm 119:10-11; John 15:3). No one is born again without the Word of God either spoken or written to him.

"Being born again, not of corruptible seed, but of incorruptible, by the word of God, which liveth and abideth forever" (1 Peter 1:23; see Romans 10:17). This passage in 1 Peter points out that man is not born again of corruptible seed which produced life at the first birth and from which each person inherits the decay of sin. Now, God says the new birth is a new life which comes from incorruptible seed which is the Word of God. The life which comes forth from this incorruptible seed is eternal life: we are adopted into God's family as His children through our faith in His Son, the Lord Jesus Christ.

When energy forms are changed you change your burner. A furnace is changed from burning coal to burning oil by putting in a conversion kit. You have to put in a conversion kit any time you change your energy. This is what happens when we leave human power and start running on divine power. The manufacturer, who happens to be God, is ready to give us a conversion experience kit so we can have His power and His energy. This is what Jesus was talking about when he said, "Marvel not that I said unto thee, Ye must be born again" (John 3:7).

The Lord Jesus went on to say in John 3:8 that the work of the Holy Spirit in saving men is like the wind. It cannot be seen, nor can its power and work be fully understood. Yet, we hear it, and it is very powerful. Jesus is saying that we see the effect of the wind, but cannot tell its source, and so it is of everyone who is born of the Holy Spirit. A definite change takes place in the person's life through the Holy Spirit's ministry, but we may not understand the method of the new birth.

Nicodemus did not understand this sort of talk and he kept asking questions (John 3:9). How was it possible for a person to be able to start life all over again? It was beyond his understanding. The whole idea seemed impossible. It is interesting to note that in John 3:11 as the Lord Jesus replies to Nicodemus's question, He used the plural when speaking, "We speak that we do know, and testify that we have seen; and ye receive not our witness."

In John 7:16-17 the Lord Jesus again emphasizes His oneness with God, "My teaching is not really mine but comes from the One who sent me. If anyone wants to do God's will, he will know whether my teaching is from God or whether I merely speak on my own authority." In many places in the Bible the Lord Jesus Christ emphasized the oneness of the Father, the Son and the Holy Ghost. "Go ye therefore, and teach all nations, baptizing them in the name of the Father, and of the Son, and of the Holy Ghost" (Matthew 28:19). (See John 14:26; 15:26; 2 Corinthians 13:14; 1 Peter 1:2.)

An Object Lesson for Nicodemus

Next, the Lord Jesus gave this ruler of the Jews an object lesson (John 3:14-16). Nicodemus was learned in the Old Testament Scriptures, and these Scriptures were the source of what Jesus taught. Nicodemus knew exactly what Jesus Christ made reference to when He spoke of Moses lifting up a serpent in the wilderness.

The story is recorded in Numbers 21:6-9. The Israelites were complaining about what God was doing with them. The Lord sent serpents among the people. Those who were bitten by the snakes died. The Israelites realized that they had sinned, and they came to Moses. "We have sinned," they confessed, "pray unto the Lord, that He take away the serpents from us."

Moses prayed and the Lord heard. "Make thee a fiery serpent," God told Moses. "Set it upon a pole: and it shall come to pass, that every one that is bitten, when he looketh upon it, shall live." Moses did as God said, and the people were healed of the plague.

Nothing less than a complete change of heart and nature, a change so complete and radical that it can only be described as a new birth, can make a person acceptable to God.

Jesus Christ told Nicodemus that the serpent of brass was a picture or type of Himself. Just as Moses put the serpent on a pole and lifted it up for the people to see, so Jesus Christ would be placed on a cross and lifted up for people to see. When the Israelites looked in faith on the brazen serpent, God healed them. When anyone looks in faith on Jesus Christ dying for him, God forgives that person's sins.

Jesus said to Nicodemus, "Ye must be born again." It was not, "I hope you will." It was not, "It will be a good thing." It was not, "I would suggest that you seek it." It was, "Ye must be born again." Nothing less than a complete change of heart and nature, a change so complete and radical that it can only be described as a new birth, can make a person acceptable to God.

Spiritual Life Is Needed

Plutarch once described a man who busied himself trying to make a corpse stand upright, but it continually fell down. Finally in disgust, he walked away saying to himself, "There's something lacking inside." There *was* something lacking inside! It was life that was lacking! The same thing is lacking inside of people, which makes them fall down morally and spiritually. The thing that is lacking is life, spiritual life, the life that God gives when a person is born again through faith in Jesus Christ.

John Green left the college campus and went down to the east side of London, where people committed every kind of sin. He was an idealist and began to set up libraries, teach classes and tried to change people. He encouraged them to paint and clean up their homes and streets. For ten years he tried, and finally gave it up. He said, "It's no use. They will go on drinking, and gambling, and stealing, and fighting until the end of time." He went back to Oxford and wrote a history of England.

Into the same wretched east side of London went General Booth of the Salvation Army. He took his Bible and preached the cross, lifting up Jesus Christ and calling men to turn from their sins to Jesus. What happened? New life! As people came in faith to Jesus Christ, lives were changed. Drunkards were made sober; thieves were made honest. Gamblers were made respectable citizens. People stopped their fighting. Homes were transformed and neighborhoods were changed.

Why did the one succeed, while the other failed? One went, trying to change people who still had sinful hearts. The other went, with the Good News of Jesus Christ, who changed their sinful hearts and lives. Individuals cannot be changed apart from a new birth, and society itself cannot be changed until there are enough people who have experienced this heart transformation. Society has many needs, but society's greatest need is for each individual to have a new heart from Jesus Christ. Jesus said it to Nicodemus and He says it to all of us, "Ye must be born again."

Only Faith Can Save Us

Unfortunately there are many people in the world today who attempt to gain God's favor by good works, church membership and a fine reputation. As good as these things may be in themselves, they have nothing to do with obtaining God's forgiveness and salvation. It is all by faith in Christ. Unfortunately there are many who are mixed up and do not understand, as Nicodemus did not understand Jesus' words.

The story is told of the mixed up bird who found a doorknob—the antique white porcelain kind—and had mistaken it for an egg. She was missed from the flock for several days and finally located in a tuft of grass squatting firmly on her porcelain prize! She probably would be sitting there today if she hadn't been robbed of her unhatchable "egg." You smile and say, "How dumb can a chicken be!" Yet, many people believe that religion can save, good works can save, while the Bible is clear on the subject that it is only faith that can save us.

Thousands of people imagine that they can earn their salvation by good works or religious exercises. No matter how "good" these efforts are they are only "white doorknobs." "For by grace (unearned love) are ye saved through faith; and that not of yourselves: it is the gift of God: not of works, lest any man should boast" (Ephesians 2:8,9). *Salvation is not "try" but "trust"; it is not "do" but "done!"— Corrie ten Boom.*

The Last Words of John the Baptist
John 3:22-36

The story of Nicodemus and Jesus ends abruptly. The Bible does not tell us what happened after these words of Jesus. We do not know what Nicodemus said or did. The conversation was over and the narrative moves on.

Once more John the Baptist comes into the picture. This is the last testimony of John concerning Christ that this Gospel gives to us. John the Baptist was continuing to baptize the people who came to him. He had moved from Bethabara where Jesus had been baptized to Aenon (John 1:28, John 3:23). Some of John's disciples were disturbed because they saw the popularity of their leader dwindling. The popularity of a new leader, Jesus Christ, was gaining. John's disciples came to him with their problem (John 3:26-30). Certainly there must have been a temptation for John the Baptist to be jealous. Yet, as we read John 3:30, we realize that he was not jealous as he said, "He must increase, but I must decrease." In answer to their complaints, it would have been very easy for John to feel neglected and forgotten.

John told his disciples three things: He told them he never expected anything else (John 3:27,28). John also told them that no man could receive more than what God gave him (John 3:27). Last of all John used a very vivid picture which portrayed Jesus as the bridegroom and himself as the friend of the bridegroom (John 3:29). Every Jewish person would recognize what he meant by this illustration.

One of the great pictures of the Old Testament is the picture of Israel as the bride of God, and God as the bridegroom of Israel. God identified so closely with the Israelites, that it could only be likened to a wedding. When Israel worshipped strange gods, it was as if she had been guilty of adultery (Exodus 34:15; Deuteronomy 31:16; Psalm 73:27; Isaiah 54:5). After Christ had come to earth, the Christians took over this picture and spoke of the Church as the bride of Christ (2 Corinthians 11:2; Ephesians 5:22-32). It was this picture that was in John's mind. Jesus had come from God. Jesus was the Son of God. Israel was His rightful bride, and He was Israel's bridegroom. John claimed for himself the privilege of being a friend of the bridegroom.

In a Jewish wedding the friend of the bridegroom had a unique position. He arranged the wedding, gave out the invitations and presided as a "master of ceremonies" at the wedding feast. John the Baptist's job had been to bring Israel and Jesus together, and to arrange the marriage between Christ (the bridegroom) and Israel (the bride). It had been his job to call Israel to repentance for sin, and prepare them to come in faith to Jesus Christ (Matthew 3:1-12; Mark 1:1-8; Luke 3:2-17). *John's task was completed,* and now he was happy to say that Jesus must increase and he must decrease.

The secret of John's joy in the Lord Jesus Christ's ministry was his recognition that " a man can receive nothing, except it be given him from heaven" (John 3:27). Later in John 3:31-35 he again speaks of the Father who loves His Son, and has given all into His hands. He also says that "God giveth not the Spirit by measure unto him." In other words, God gave everything freely to the Lord Jesus Christ— there is no limit. John showed only joy in the truths that he expressed; there was no sign of envy. If every Christian could remember that each man receives from heaven what God wants to give, there would be no conflict due to pride and envy among God's children. If God is the giver of every gift, God will give exactly the right gift to each Christian.

There is another important must in John 3:30 "He must grow greater and greater and I less and less." Is this happening in your life? Are you allowing the Lord Jesus to speak to you daily in a time of prayer and the reading of His precious Word, the Bible? Do you consider His will when you make decisions? As Jesus Christ becomes more and more important, the decision to do what you know He wants you to do, becomes easier and easier. Ask Him to help you to say, "I want your way more and my way less." Be willing to be like John the Baptist who was happy to be forgotten if Christ was remembered. The Lord Jesus Christ, by the power of the Holy Spirit, is waiting to help you today.

Study Questions

Before you begin your study this week:
1. Pray each day and ask God to speak to you through His Holy Spirit.
2. Use only your Bible to answer the following questions.
3. Write down your answers and, where called for, include the verses you used.
4. Challenge questions are for those who have the time and who wish to do them.
5. Personal questions are to be shared with your study group only if you wish to share.
6. As you study, look for a verse to memorize this week. Write it down, carry it with you, tack it to your bulletin board, tape it to the dashboard of your car. Make a real effort to learn the verse and its reference.

FIRST DAY: Read all of the preceding notes and look up all of the Scriptures given.

1. What was a helpful or new thought from the overview of John 3?

2. What personal application did you select to apply to your own life?

SECOND DAY: Read all of John 4 concentrating on verses 1-6.

1. Who baptized those who came in faith to the Lord Jesus?

2. What had the Pharisees (Jewish religious leaders) heard about the Lord Jesus?

3 a. Where did the Lord Jesus go after He left Judea? Find these places on your Bible map if possible.

b. What area did the Lord Jesus travel through on this journey and in what city did He stop?

c. What important event had taken place near this city many years before?

4 a. At about noon (the sixth hour) where did Jesus and His disciples arrive?

b. How does John 4:6 express how the Lord Jesus felt at this time?

5. Challenge: Read Philippians 2:5-11 and record the facts you find about Christ Jesus.

6 a. Which verse in Philippians 2:5-11 expressed to you the Lord Jesus Christ's special love to you?

b. (Personal) Have you ever shown your love for the Lord Jesus by doing what Philippians 2:10-11 describes? If not, perhaps today is the day you will choose to respond in love to His love.

c. Have you underlined in your Bible your favorite verses in Philippians 2:5-11? This is a good way to help you remember them and find them again.

THIRD DAY: Read John 4:7-15.

1. Whom did Jesus ask to draw Him a drink of water from the well and what was this person's response?

2. What does Jesus Christ say about the "living water" which God is willing to give to those who ask for it? Give verse.

3. **Challenge:** How do the following verses help you to understand "living water" which the Lord Jesus offers? Use your own words if you wish to.

   John 7:37-39

   Revelation 21:6

4. How does Isaiah 12:2-3 seem to relate to "living water?"

5. and 6. How can you personally do what the last half of Isaiah 12:3 suggests? Give as many thoughts on how a Christian could do this as you can.

FOURTH DAY: Read John 4:16-26.

1 a. What did the woman admit to Jesus Christ about her husband? Give verse.

   b. What did He tell her about her life?

2. Since the Lord Jesus knew all about her life, who did she think He was?

3. How did she try to change the subject from her personal sin to another subject in John 4:20?

4 a. How did the woman try to show Jesus that she was knowledge-able about spiritual things in John 4:25?

   b. What claim to His deity did the Lord Jesus make at this time?

5. How does Philippians 3:3 help you to understand John 4:24 more fully? Put into your own words if you can.

6 a. **Challenge:** Read all of 2 Peter 3:17-18. As we rejoice in the Lord Jesus what is the Christian to "beware of" in these verses and what is the Christian to "grow in"?

b. (Personal) How do you believe you can "grow" as a Christian? Try to list some things you want the Lord to help you "grow" in this week.

FIFTH DAY: Read John 4:27-42.

1 a. What was the reaction of the disciples when they found the Lord Jesus talking to a woman?

 b. **Challenge:** Do you believe that a woman is "liberated" by Christ or by legislation? If possible give some reasons and Scriptures with your answer.

2 a. Where did this woman go and what did she say?

 b. What was the people's reaction to this woman's words according to John 4:30?

 c. Describe the result of the woman telling people about the Lord Jesus and their going to the city well to see Him. See John 4:39.

 d. **Challenge:** Have you ever told anyone about the Lord Jesus Christ and seen the same results? How would you tell someone about Him? What Scripture verses would you choose to use?

3 a. How long did the Lord Jesus stay and teach these people?

b. Did any more people believe after He stayed and taught them?

c. What did these people say they knew about the Lord Jesus after hearing His words? Give verse.

4. **Challenge:** What do the following verses say about the Word of God? Put them into your own words if you are able to.

Mark 13:31

Romans 10:17

5. Which of the above verses was your favorite? Why did you choose it?

6. (Personal) Has John 4:42 ever become an experience of reality in your life? Have you ever responded as these people did? See John 4:25-26.

SIXTH DAY: Read John 4:27-54.

1. How did the Lord Jesus respond when the disciples urged Him to eat the food they had brought to the well from Sychar? Give verse.

2. How do the following verses help you to understand this food that the Lord Jesus Christ spoke of?

Matthew 4:4

Jeremiah 3:15

3. What did the Lord Jesus say was His "meat" in John 4? Give verse.

4 a. **Challenge:** How does Hebrews 1:1-3 help explain who Jesus Christ is and also tell what His work on earth was? Find as many details as you can in these three verses.

   b. (Personal) Which of these thoughts about the Lord Jesus and His work was the most interesting or thought provoking to you? Share these thoughts with someone if possible.

5. What was the second sign that Jesus Christ did, which John recorded, to show that He was indeed the Messiah?

6. Which verse did you choose to hide in your heart as "secret food" for your life? Try repeating a verse at least five times daily if you want to memorize it.

COME TO THE LIVING WATERS!

John 4

Study Notes

Jesus Offers the Water of Life John 4:1-26

The Jewish people, in the days of Christ, held a grudge against the Samaritans. Sometimes a grudge can get so out of hand that rather foolish things result.

The Samaritans came into being after the kingdom of Israel fell to the Assyrians in 722 B.C. They were the children of the Israelites who remained in Israel, and Assyrian exiles who had been placed in Samaria by the king of Assyria (2 Kings 17:24-27). The Samaritans were hated by the Jews because they had intermarried, and also because they had opposed the rebuilding of the Temple at Jerusalem (Ezra 4). The Samaritan woman mentioned in the controversy in John 4:20 and John 4:9 indicates that the Jews still had no dealings with the Samaritans. The woman was surprised when a Jewish man asked her for a drink of water.

The grudge between the two groups had become so bad that the Jews would not even cross through the land of Samaria. Instead they would cross the River Jordan and travel along the east side of the river until they got opposite the province they wanted to visit. The land of Palestine is only 120 miles long from north to south, but at the time of Jesus there were three divisions within this territory: Galilee was in the north, Judea at the extreme south, and Samaria lay in between. Obviously, the quickest route from Galilee to Judea would be directly through Samaria, a journey of three days. The alternate route across the Jordan took twice as long.

In John 4:4 we read, "And he had to pass through Samaria." Why did Jesus Christ have to go through Samaria? Certainly, not just because He wanted to go from Judea to Galilee! He could have taken the usual route along the east side of the river. He had to go through Samaria because He had to talk to a woman who needed Him.

This is the only record we have that Jesus Christ visited Samaria during His ministry. He stopped at the well outside of Sychar because He was "wearied with his journey" (John 4:6). It had been a long walk from Judea to Sychar, and Jesus stopped just outside the town where the road to Samaria forks off to three other small towns. Just at the fork of the road there still stands a well which is known as Jacob's well.

The well itself, at that time, was more than 100 feet deep and is not supplied by a spring, but water seeps into it and settles in the well. The well is so deep that no one can get water from it without something with which to draw it out.

Many historical Jewish events took place in this area. Jacob bought a piece of ground (Genesis 33:18-19). On his death bed he gave this land to Joseph (Genesis 48:22). When Joseph died in Egypt, his body was taken back to Palestine and buried on this land (Joshua 24:32).

It was about the sixth hour (noon) and Jesus sat down to rest for He was tired from the journey (John 4:6). Imagine, the Son of God was tired! That was a new experience for the One who had made the world.

The Lord Jesus Christ could have been tempted to ignore the Samaritan woman's need because He was tired. It's certainly a common emotion each one of us has experienced when we feel weary; but the Lord Jesus Christ promised to give us His love, compassion and strength to share with someone in need even when we feel weary. "Because he himself suffered when he was tempted, he is able to help those who are being tempted" (Hebrews 2:18).

Jesus Christ set an example for us by unselfishly humbling Himself, leaving His heavenly home and coming to earth; taking the form of a servant, being born like a man, He was perfect God, perfect Man. He humbled Himself and was obedient even unto death on the cross for our sakes (Phil. 2:5-11). Our response to His love should be to humble ourselves before God, and use our time and energy for His purpose.

America's famous Giant Springs can be seen only at Great Falls, Montana. In the spiritual realm Giant Springs should be found flowing wherever you find true believers in the Lord Jesus Christ (John 7:38). In the dry, thirsty, barren land of this world, is your life a refreshment and blessing to others? Has the Holy Spirit taken complete control of you? (Romans 8:1, Romans 12:1-2). Today, allow the Holy Spirit to fill you until you become a Giant Spring of living water.

CLOWN FACES

Dear Lord,
    my little one cuddles in my arms
        and says
            Let me paint a clown face
            on you, Mommy.

It was her own idea;
    no one taught her this little game
    but we play it often together.

She paints my face in imaginary colors
    and I paint hers in turn.
        We play this pointless little game
        over and over again.

Lord, grown up people play this
    in their game of life too.
        They paint on a smiling face
            so that the world can't see the
                fear,
                    sadness,
                        defeat,
                            misery,
                                bitterness,
                                    and emptiness
                                    in their hearts.

Please, dear Lord, help me
    to see behind these grown-up clown faces.
        Show me the need of each heart
            that you send across my path
            by your Holy Spirit.

And Lord, I ask you to show me
    how to help them
        drop their clown faces
            and reach out for YOU.

                                    Doris Greig

But God protected me so that I am still alive today to tell these facts to everyone, both great and small. I teach nothing except what the prophets and Moses said—That the Messiah would suffer, and be the First to rise from the dead, to bring light to Jews and Gentiles alike. (Acts 26:22-23)

The Woman of Samaria

As the Lord Jesus Christ sat by the well alone, His disciples went into the city to buy food (John 4:8). While sitting there, a woman of Samaria came to draw water. She probably was carrying the water pot upon her shoulder or head. She may have walked 45 minutes down a rocky path to this age-old well, that still is used today, to get her daily supply of water.

The village itself was up on a hill, where early inhabitants found protection from their enemies. The people daily visited Jacob's well for their water. Traditionally, the women went to the well early in the morning while the sun was low in the sky, but this woman was not accepted by the other women so she came alone in the heat of the day to get her water.

The barriers between the Jews and the Samaritans had already been shaken because the Jewish disciples had gone into Sychar to buy food—an unusual occurrence for the village. Soon the barrier will completely fall as Jesus' words build the bridge of God's love to this woman.

Jesus begins by asking her to give Him a drink of water. She must have been amazed and surprised that a Jewish man would even speak to her, as no man had probably spoken like a gentleman to her for a long time. She was the village prostitute, was probably hated by the women and no gentleman of Samaria would want to be seen speaking to her. In Jesus' words, she seems to immediately sense someone who does not condemn her, but someone who understands her need.

Shouldn't this be our attitude to those who are separated from God? We need to reach out with loving words and hands and draw them into the arms of the Savior. We are to be "channels of blessings" for Him. Do you always act as willingly and promptly as your Lord did at this time? Is there someone walking or working near you who needs to know the Savior?

Jesus Elevates Woman's Status

Another barrier which the Lord Jesus broke down was that of greeting a woman in public, particularly a Samaritan woman. A rabbi was not even allowed to speak to his own wife, daughter or sister in public! One group of Pharisees was called "the bruised and bleeding Pharisees." Because they shut their eyes when they saw a woman on the street, they bumped into walls and houses! If a rabbi was seen speaking to a woman in public, he lost his reputation. Yet Jesus spoke to this woman of notorious character in public.

This was the Son of God who was tired, weary and thirsty. Jesus was the holiest of men, who listened to a sad story with understanding. It was Jesus Christ Himself who gave women a place of honor in society. As they came to Him for forgiveness of their sins, they became joint heirs with Jesus Christ (through their faith). "There is neither Jew nor Greek, there is neither bond nor free, there is neither male nor female: for ye are all one in Christ Jesus" (Galatians 3:28).

The Holy Spirit will constantly flood your life with joy and power as the living water of the Lord Jesus Christ is manifested in your life through Him.

Perhaps you find yourself identifying with the Samaritan woman in this story. She had no reputation and no friends; she was lonely and had many needs. Perhaps you have lost everything you cherished that seemed valuable to you. The Lord Jesus wants to share with you the same thing He offered to this woman—"'If you only knew what a wonderful gift God has for you, and who I am, you would ask me for some living water!' . . . People soon become thirsty again after drinking this water [from the well]. 'But the water I give them,' he said, 'becomes a perpetual spring within them, watering them forever with eternal life'" (John 4:10,13-14). The Lord Jesus Christ wants us to come to Him in faith as this woman did, and He will fill us with the "perpetual spring" of "living water" which He has promised to those who believe in Him. The Holy Spirit will constantly flood your life with joy and power as the living water of the Lord Jesus Christ is manifested in your life through Him (John 7:38-39).

"But when the time came for the kindness and love of God our Savior to appear, then he saved us—not because we were good enough to be saved, but because of his kindness and pity—by washing away our sins and giving us the new joy of the indwelling Holy Spirit whom he poured out upon us with wonderful fullness—and all because of what Jesus Christ our Savior did so that he could declare us good in God's eyes—all because of his great kindness" (Titus 3:4-7).

Desert Pete's Well

The following letter was found many years ago in a tin tied to an old pump on a remote desert trail: "This pump is all right as of June 1932. I put a new sucker washer into it and it ought to last five years. But the washer dries out and pump has got to be primed. Under the white rock I buried a bottle of water, out of the sun and cork end up. There's enough water in it to prime the pump, but not if you drink some first. Pour about one fourth and let her soak to wet the leather. Then pour in the rest medium fast and pump like crazy. You'll get water. The well has never run dry. Have faith. When you get watered up, fill the bottle, and put it back as you found it for the next feller. Desert Pete."

Imagine the year is 1936 and you are an exhausted, thirsty and desperate desert traveler. You come to Desert Pete's well. Would you drink the minimal supply of water and forget the unlimited supply supposedly in the well? Or would you risk your life and empty the water into the pump in order to gain an adequate supply? The unthinking person would probably consume the bottled water.

Thinking man sees the issue: faith, risk and a promise of life, or doubt, temporary relief and a certainty of death. But can he believe? He has to consider the object of faith. He must believe that Desert Pete is a real person and not a figment of the imagination. There is not strict proof of this, but the evidence of the tin, the letter and the bottle under the white rock points in this direction.

But was Desert Pete's character reliable? His reliability can be tested if the bottle is under the rock. If it is, you can presume that Desert Pete is a good reliable man. Now comes the step of faith—a commitment to Desert Pete and his word. You are gloriously rewarded! The pump works, and the cool, saving flow of water is the proof.

Springs of Living Water

In another desert is another well and another Word—the Bible. In this Word of God is this promise, "Everyone who drinks this water will thirst again, but whoever drinks the water I give him will never thirst. Indeed, the water I give him will become in him a spring of water welling up to eternal life" (John 4:13-14). Now, traveler, *you* stand at the well. What are you going to do? "And this is the record, that God hath given to us eternal life, and this life is in his Son" (1 John 5:11). "He that believeth in me, though he were dead, yet shall he live: And whosoever liveth and believeth in me shall never die" (John 11:25-26).

"Drink the water I give you, and you will never thirst again," Jesus said. Such words seemed more than the woman could imagine. She had so many needs. Here was a man who claimed that He could supply them all. Of course she wanted that water! But she also wanted to get away from the necessity of coming every day to draw water (John 4:15).

Jesus came right to the point. "Go call your husband," He said. This was a touchy subject to this Samaritan woman, for she had had many husbands, and the man whom she was living with was not her own. She tried to dodge the question (John 4:17). However, Jesus knew the truth (John 4:18). The woman wanted to change the subject by getting into an age-old argument about the place to worship.

The Samaritans had built their own temple on Mount Gerizim. Here they went to worship, not to the Temple of Jerusalem. The Lord Jesus told the woman that the place of worship was not as important as the act of worship (John 4:23-24). The woman tried to get involved in an argument about a place of worship because she did not want to talk about her own need for a Savior. The Lord Jesus answered her question simply.

Then she tried again by getting into a discussion about the coming Messiah. Again the Lord had an answer for her. This answer was even more amazing to her than the last one!

The woman said, "'Well, at least I know that the Messiah will come—the one they call Christ—and when he does, he will explain everything to us.'"

Then Jesus told her, "'I am the Messiah!'" (John 4:25-26).

The Disciples Return from Sychar
John 4:31-38

The Lord Jesus and the woman had been alone when this discussion took place. At the end of the conversation the disciples returned from the city where they had gone to buy food (John 4:8). They were amazed when they saw Jesus speaking with a woman, and more amazed to find Him no longer hungry. He explained that doing the will of God—meeting the needs of poor sinners like this woman—was more to Him than food. He challenged them to look around. The people of Samaria were hungry for the gospel. They were like grain waiting to be harvested (John 4:31-35).

Speaking to the woman and bringing her into a realization of who Jesus is was His mission. It should be ours as well. Are you willing to ask the Lord to send someone your way with whom you can share the Good News of Jesus Christ? How important is witnessing for Christ in your life? Have you ever given up something you wanted to do in order to speak to somebody about the Lord Jesus?

Have you wondered why the Lord Jesus referred to the hills as being "white unto harvest?" He and His disciples arrived at the well at the sixth hour, which is noon. Perhaps as He stood with the disciples facing Him, He could see the hillside with the village at the top, and see men and women winding their way down the path to Jacob's well after the woman had run to the village to proclaim her good news (John 4:28-29). As He watched this mass of people moving down the hillside, He thought aloud about the harvest of souls and compared it to the harvest of the crop that was still four months away. Thus, He said to His disciples, "Lift up your eyes, and look on the fields," and the disciples looked and saw the people coming down the hill to see the One this prostitute had spoken of so glowingly (John 4:35).

The fact that the woman left her water pot (John 4:28) and went to the city, showed that her heart was anxious to share the good news which she had just received. She proclaimed her faith as she said, "Come, see a man who told me everything I ever did. Could this be the Christ?" (John 4:29). She knew that the people of her village had observed her in her sinful ways and knew all that she had ever done, but not this man who was a stranger to her. Now she proclaimed that He indeed must be the Messiah for whom they had been looking.

Her life illustrates what the Christian life should be. It should be like twin pillars called "Discovery" and "Communication." No true discovery is complete without the desire to share the excitement and joy of it with others. Yet we cannot communicate our faith in Christ to others until we have discovered Him!

The Conversion of the Samaritans
John 4:39-42

When the Samaritans of Sychar heard the woman's testimony, they hurried to the well to hear Jesus speak and asked Him to stay for two days with them (John 4:39-40). They heard, they believed and they wanted to learn more. The belief of the people went beyond the testimony of the woman (John 4:41-42). They came to Christ and heard Him themselves and trusted Him as a result of what they heard Him say.

In John 4:42 they gave Jesus a new title—"Savior of the World." This is the first time that Jesus had gone to any group other than Jews, and is the first time He is called the "Savior of the World." No wonder the Bible records that Jesus "had to go through Samaria" (John 4:4)!

Jesus Performs His Second Miracle
John 4:43-54

After two days, the Lord Jesus departed for Galilee with His disciples. All three other Gospels tell of Jesus saying that a prophet has no

78

honor in his own country (Matthew 13:57; Mark 6:4; Luke 4:24). The saying was an ancient proverb which the people used in the same way that we say, "Familiarity breeds contempt."

When Jesus arrived in Galilee, the people welcomed Him for they had seen how He had cleansed the Temple in Jerusalem at the feast (John 2:13-25). Every Jewish person over 19 years of age who went to the Passover feast had to pay the Temple tax, so that the Temple sacrifices and the Temple ritual could be carried out daily. This tax was one half shekel, the equivalent of about two days' wages, a great deal for these people to give for the Lord's service. Ordinarily any kind of currency was usable in trade in Palestine, but the Temple tax had to be paid in either Galilean or sanctuary shekels. These were Jewish coins, the only ones acceptable for a special gift to the sanctuary.

Since Jewish believers arrived from all over the world with all kinds of coins, the Temple courts were filled with money changers who took advantage of the pilgrims by overcharging them for the exchange of coins. There were also inspectors within the Temple grounds inspectors who examined and determined if the animals sold for sacrifice were perfect.

The Lord Jesus Christ cares about inequities in our society and is offended by those who take advantage of the poor and helpless.

It was this social injustice and dishonesty which Jesus took action against when He cleansed the Temple in John 2. Undoubtedly this is why we read in John 4:45 that the Galileans welcomed Him, for they had seen that He cared about their personal welfare when He cleansed the Temple at the time of the Passover feast. The Lord Jesus Christ also cares about inequities in our society and is offended by those who take advantage of the poor and helpless.

In the last verses of this chapter John records another miracle or sign (John 4:46-54). The nobleman was an official, either civil or military, in the service of Herod, the King. However, when his son was sick, his position did not help him. Notice, as soon as Jesus said that the boy would live, the man believed. When the nobleman arrived home and saw that the Lord's word was true, he and his whole house believed in Jesus Christ.

The Bible records, "The man believed the word that Jesus had spoken unto him" (John 4:50). He had only the word of the Lord. He was not with his son, so he could not see that anything had been done. Yet he took Christ at His word. We need to trust the Lord Jesus Christ to supply our needs in this same way. He can!

Study Questions

Before you begin your study this week:

1. Pray each day and ask God to speak to you through His Holy Spirit.
2. Use only your Bible to answer the following questions.
3. Write down your answers and, where called for, include the verses you used.
4. Challenge questions are for those who have the time and who wish to do them.
5. Personal questions are to be shared with your study group only if you wish to share.
6. As you study, look for a verse to memorize this week. Write it down, carry it with you, tack it to your bulletin board, tape it to the dashboard of your car. Make a real effort to learn the verse and its reference.

FIRST DAY: Read all of the preceding notes and look up all of the Scriptures given.

1. What was a helpful or new thought from the Overview of John 4?

2. What personal application did you select to apply to your own life?

SECOND DAY: Read all of John 5 concentrating on 5:1-16.

1 a. Where did the Lord Jesus go after He left Cana of Galilee (John 4:46)?

b. Describe the place in Jerusalem where the Lord Jesus went.

c. What kind of people did the Lord Jesus find at this place?

2. List all of the things you can discover about the condition and life of the man that Jesus singled out to heal.

3 a. What did the Lord Jesus ask the man to do? Was the man obedient?

   b. (Personal) Has the Lord Jesus asked you to do anything as you have read His Word in the study of John this year? Have you been obedient to His Word?

   c. What does Ephesians 6:6-7 say the attitude of the Christian should be concerning obedience to God?

   d. (Personal) Is this your heart attitude of obedience to God? Should you pray and ask God to help you change your attitude? Psalm 57:2 and Romans 12:12 are helpful.

4. **Challenge:** The lame man was made whole physically by Jesus Christ. Compare this wholeness to the forgiveness, cleansing from sin, and wholeness a person receives when he comes in faith to Jesus Christ as Lord and Savior.

5. Compare Galatians 5:16-24 with Jesus Christ's statement in John 5:11,14. Does this help you with Question 4?

81

6. Look up Galatians 2:19-20, preferably in a modern language translation such as *The Living Bible*. Put your name in the place of "I" as you write out this verse. Choose to ask the Lord to make this verse "come alive" in your life this week.

THIRD DAY: Read John 5:16-23.

1. Why did the Jewish people seek to persecute Jesus and kill him? Give verses.

2. What does this passage tell you about God the Father? Give verses.

3. What does this passage tell you about Jesus Christ the Son?

4. What does this passage say that our attitude is to be both to God the Father and God the Son?

5. **Challenge:** Explain in your own words how you feel a person can "honor" God the Father and God the Son.

6 a. Challenge: How do the following verses suggest ways of honoring God the Father and God the Son?

Psalm 29:2

Isaiah 25:1

Philippians 3:7-9

b. Which of these verses meant the most to you? Share the reason if possible.

FOURTH DAY: Read John 5:24-27.

1 **a.** If we hear the words of Jesus and believe on Him what does He promise us in John 5:24?

b. (Personal) Do you have what John 5:24 promises because of your faith in Jesus Christ? See Acts 4:12 and Romans 1:16-17.

2. How does John 14:6 relate to John 5:26?

3. What does John 5:27 say God has given Jesus Christ authority to do?

4. Challenge: What do the following verses say about Jesus Christ as judge?

Acts 10:38-42

Romans 2:16

Romans 14:10

2 Timothy 4:1

5. Second Timothy 4:1 speaks of Jesus Christ judging people when He returns to earth. His second coming is foretold in many places in the Scriptures. Choose some of the following verses concerning His second coming. Write down your favorites. Acts 1:11, Hebrews 9:28, Matthew 16:27, Matthew 25:31-32, 1 Corinthians 4:5, Matthew 24:44, 1 Thessalonians 5:23.

6. Which of the above verses gave you the most joy, hope or challenge in your life? Why?

FIFTH DAY: Read John 5:28-39.

1. Whose will did the Lord Jesus always seek as He walked this earth as perfect God—perfect Man?

2. Compare John 5:32 with John 5:37. Who is it that bears witness of Jesus Christ to us?

3. These are three other "witnesses" for Jesus Christ which He talks about here other than God the Father. What are the three other witnesses given in this passage? Give verses.

4. After Jesus Christ's death, resurrection, and ascension, what other witness also pointed men to the Savior? See Acts 14:17.

5. How does Romans 1:20 add to the thoughts of Acts 14:17?

6 a. **Challenge:** Since all men have been given some witness of God's love, do you believe that anyone can be "neutral" about God? Is there a "gray area" or is man either in the darkness of sin (Romans 3:23) or the light of His love (Romans 6:23)?

   b. Are you sharing the "good news" of Jesus Christ with those of your acquaintance? Do you believe that God wants you to be His witness? How can you be His witness?

SIXTH DAY: Read John 5:39-47.

1. List the things that you find in these verses that must have broken Jesus Christ's heart. He had come to offer all people forgiveness and eternal life, and they refused to receive this free gift. Give verses with your answer.

2. Do you believe that Jesus Christ's heart is still breaking today because man will not respond in faith to Him, but respond in the same way as described in this part of John 5?

3. (Personal) How have you responded to Jesus Christ? Do you believe His words? See John 5:47.

4. God's Word is His communication to you today. How do the following Scriptures help you understand how important it is for you to read and meditate upon His Word? Put them into your own words if possible.

   2 Timothy 3:16

   2 Peter 1:20-21

5. **Challenge:** What action is the Christian to take concerning God's Word? Write down what is suggested in each of the following verses.

   Psalm 78:5-7

   Psalm 119:11

6 a. How can you let "Christ's Word" dwell richly in you in all wisdom (Colossians 3:16)? Name some practical ways.

   b. Did you choose to memorize some favorite portion of Scripture this week?

THE LIFE-GIVING POWER OF JESUS

John 5

Study Notes

Jesus Heals the Lame Man John 5:1-16

The Lord Jesus Christ constantly surprises people around Him. In the first four chapters of John we discovered Him changing water to wine, chasing animals and people out of the Temple area, telling Nicodemus that he must be born again, going through Samaria and healing a boy whom He never saw.

The Lord is now in the second year of His ministry, and according to John 5:1, He moves out of Galilee again. Jerusalem is on a hill so John rightly describes Jesus as going "up" to Jerusalem. The Lord Jesus went to the pool of Bethesda, near the sheep gate where the sheep market was located. The place of the miracle is now identified with confidence following the excavation in 1888 of such a pool as John described, located in the northeastern part of Jerusalem. Archeologists uncovered five porches, which sheltered a great many sick people who lay around the pool on these porches, hoping to be healed when the water was troubled (John 5:3).

"The moving of the water could be the activity of angels, for there are unseen energies and powers sent by God which operate for the healing of man. God could also use an intermittent spring to bring healing. But let us not lose sight of the greatest miracle! The man immediately became well through the power of Jesus Christ (John 5:9).

Jesus had gone to Jerusalem alone as no mention is made of His disciples in this chapter. As He walked along the porches and saw the people, He looked at one man who was lying there. The man was lame and could not walk for he had been sick 38 years (John 5:5).

Undoubtedly many of the others who were suffering had friends with them to lower them into the water when it became "troubled," but Jesus noticed that this man was all alone. Others had friends to help them while he had "no man" (John 5:7).

One can sense this man's feeling of helplessness and despair as Jesus asks him, "Would you like to get well?" "I can't," the sick man said, "for I have no one to help me into the pool at the movement of the water. While I am trying to get there, someone else always gets in ahead of me."

Jesus noticed his aloneness and saw his psychological need to have someone care for him. He also knew that this man needed forgiveness of sin (John 5:14) as well as physical healing. As the Lord Jesus looked at this man He said in essence, "Do you really want to be changed," by asking him, "Wilt thou be made whole?" (John 5:6).

Many people are sick physically, spiritually or psychologically, who would rather accept their condition than to cooperate with the Lord Jesus in order to be made whole! Subconsciously they may prefer to remain sick and dependent rather than be a whole person and have to fight the battles of life! You may know someone who is in a condition similar to this lame man of long ago, or perhaps you may discover that you are subconsciously preferring to be sick and helpless rather than a whole person. Perhaps you feel that no one cares about you, but remember that the Lord Jesus loves you just as much as He loved this man of long ago, and wants to give you His loving compassion and help today. (Matthew 8:17; Hebrews 13:8; Revelation 1:5.)

This story is a picture of how Christ can help any life today. Multitudes of impotent folk in the world today are waiting for God's moving of the water of life to bring healing to their souls. The Lord Jesus Christ is still asking, "Do you want to be healed?" (see John 5:6). People who are psychologically crippled, spiritually sick, discouraged and frustrated with our present world, and some who are dissatisfied with formal Christianity, need to be healed by the Lord Jesus Christ and brought into the fellowship of the Church.

Christ is the head of the Church (Romans 9:5; 1 Corinthians 11:3; Ephesians 1:10,22-23). And all who respond to Him in faith become "the church of God, which he hath purchased with his own blood" (Acts 20:28). The first part of Acts 20:28 speaks of feeding the flock over which the Holy Spirit has made Christians overseers. As a Christian this is your responsibility today! For you are God's ambassador, calling men to "be healed" by Jesus Christ's forgiveness and love (John 1:12; 2 Corinthians 6:18; Galatians 4:6; Colossians 2:10).

Are you sharing the Lord Jesus Christ with anyone? "Look! I have been standing at the door and I am constantly knocking. If anyone hears me calling him and opens the door, I will come in and fellowship with him and he with me" (Revelation 3:20). Have you ever shared this Scripture with anyone?

Chinese "House Churches"

Today many true Christian believers around the world are willing to risk their lives in order to share their faith in Jesus Christ. Most meet in "house churches" because they live in countries where freedom to worship the true and living God is limited by government rules. How are they motivated to evangelism when it means the risk of persecution of themselves and their families, and perhaps even years of imprisonment for the one who is accused of anti-government activities? Their inward strength comes from the Lord (Colossians 1:27) as they follow the same plan today that the Holy Spirit gave to the first Christian believers in Jerusalem. The house churches described in Acts 2:42-47 devoted themselves to hearing and absorbing the apostle teaching, breaking of bread together, and to prayer. All three of these guidelines for Christian growth and fellowship were important, but with prayer they had God-given power to witness to pagans living all around them!

Researchers studying the growth of the house churches in China are quoted as saying "It appears that the distinguishing feature of present day church growth in China is the disciplined prayer life of every believer." This is true of Christian believers who are undergoing persecution in many lands: persecuted believers are the prayer warriors of our day. The Chinese Christians have a motto "A little prayer; a little power." The last half of the motto is "No prayer; no power."

I would add to the Chinese motto these words: "Much prayer; much power." We need to learn from our fellow Christians who are suffering persecution. May we realize the power of prayer as we read of their examples of faith.

The South Korean Christians have also discovered the fruit of much prayer is much power from the Lord. Many Koreans whose prayer lives have deepened during suffering have seen the fruit of answered prayer as many new believers have received Christ by faith. The Koreans, like the Chinese Christians, have been called to prayer. Since the early part of the century, thousands have been going to their churches to pray daily before breakfast. Every Friday tens of thousands of Korean Christians spend the whole night in prayer in their churches. Many take their vacation to go to prayer mountains for prayer retreats, where they intercede in cubicles and find God's solutions for their problems.

Where there is such emphasis on prayer, spiritual battles are won in Christ's power, and the glory is given to Him. Could a barren prayer life be the reason why we see so little power in our own lives and in the Body of Christ? Shouldn't these Christians be living examples to challenge us to pray more often and more faithfully?

Every Saturday morning in one of China's largest and most important cities, Chinese Christians meet in a house church for a day of fasting and prayer. They begin at 9 A.M. and continue on until 3 P.M. or even later when they sense this is God's leading. They do not meet to talk about prayer. They pray—all day! In this particular group each person has spent an average of seventeen years in prison because of his faith and commitment to the Lord Jesus. Of course many other groups are praying quietly throughout all of China, and not all have been prisoners for their faith. Yet, what an example of courage these Christians are to us, who have served in prison for so many years! We let little excuses keep us from private and corporate prayer. Let's not just talk about prayer. Let's pray!

David Adeney, writing in the *World Christian Magazine,* January 1989, points out that the independent house churches in China face increased pressure from the Marxist government. These house churches could be quickly shut down by the government backed churches known as the Three Self Patriotic Movement (TSPM). During the cultural revolution the TSPM along with all other religious organizations was abolished. In the 1980s the TSPM was resurrected by the government and became the Religious Affairs Bureau (RAB). At the same time the government formed another agency to control religion called the China Christian Council (CCC).

When Adeney asked the TSPM pastor if he could give Bible study materials and commentaries he had brought to the country as gifts for the TSPM church, he was told he would have to get permission from Bishop Ding. Leaders in the house churches on the other hand were delighted with the books he had brought for them as many have only had a page or two of the Bible. They received the books as from the Lord. The door to China has opened a crack.

Four mission agencies are cooperating to produce 2,000 of these single-volume study Bibles for distribution, legally, all over China by the end of 1989. The cooperating missions say the most urgent need in China is "to try and ensure that the explosive numerical growth of believers is matched by an increase in maturity of the Christian leders."

Surely we should pray for the doors of China to remain open so the people may have these study Bibles to help them mature in Christ. If not, heresies will take their toll. Word has come out that two cults are already proselytizing in Beijing with some success. The door has been opened by the Chinese government to these non-Christian sects. We need to pray that the revival in China survives through the sound teaching of God's

Word, and that the Chinese will be protected from any cult the government may allow to enter the country.

On several occasions the TSPM has ordered the house churches to close down because they know they are standing firmly for the Lord Jesus Christ and teaching His Word to any who will listen. This does not please the TSPM government appointed ministers. Yet the house churches have stood firm and maintained their independence from the TSPM and CCC. These house churches have their own teachers and evangelists, and do not receive speakers appointed by the government, for they know that the whole counsel of God will not be preached or taught by such men ordained by the government.

Visitors to China's TSPM churches may be impressed by their large congregations and reported baptisms. What they seldom realize are the tensions that exist beneath the surface of these churches. Most pastors are theologically liberal and primarily motivated by political concerns. It is forbidden in the TSPM churches to propagate religious theology or baptize any member of the Communist Party or the Communist Youth League. No one under the age of 18 years may be taught anything about God. The seminaries where the pastors for the TSPM churches are trained are filled with government appointed professors who agree to teach only what the Communist Party permits. Because of such policies in the TSPM seminaries, the house churches have arranged secret Bible schools in remote areas, and some young people have gone to live in the home of experienced Bible teachers in order to receive sound personal tutoring.

One evangelical pastor who felt called to stay in the TSPM church told of a man who came to his church for the first time in search of a Bible. He had been converted through listening to Christian radio and had never seen a pastor before! The evangelical pastor was able to get him a Bible, but when the man got up to give his testimony in church, a government trained pastor in the church ran over and told him he must never, never mention the Christian radio ministry to anyone. Thus you see the two extremes in one TSPM church. Usually there is no evangelical minister and the people never hear the truth from the TSPM pastor. Incidentally, even the gatekeepers of the TSPM churches are government appointed. They are taught how to keep new Christians and seekers from even getting inside the church!

There will be a great day of rejoicing in heaven when all Christians stand before the throne of God! Here we will meet persecuted Christians from all ages and countries who have stood strong for our Savior. One elderly respected Chinese house church pastor was imprisoned because he had baptized 3,000 people and preached in illegal places. I'm looking forward to meeting him! We need to keep these faithful servants of God in our prayers.

In the past some Christian believers have been tortured for not revealing the names of those with whom they have associated or from whom they have received Christian literature. Would we be as willing to obediently follow where our Savior leads us? We need to choose to walk in close fellowship with our Lord and His people. We need to protest the persecution of devoted servants of Christ whose only crime is that they will not accept their atheistic government's restrictions on preaching the gospel. We need to pray for the house churches as well as those who work within the TSPM government churches. Your prayers are heard by God and He will answer them.

God never asks us to do anything without giving us the power to obey. The obedience and the power are simultaneous.

"That He would grant you, according to the riches of His glory, to be strengthened with power through His Spirit in the inner man; so that Christ may dwell in your hearts through faith; and that you, being rooted and grounded in love, may be able to comprehend with all the saints what is the breadth and length and height and depth, and to know the love of Christ which surpasses knowledge, that you may be filled up to all the fulness of God. Now to Him who is able to do exceeding abundantly beyond all that we ask or think, according to the power that works within us, to Him be the glory in the church and in Christ Jesus to all generations forever and ever. Amen" (Ephesians 3:16-21).

The Power of the Holy Spirit

Safety officials at the Oakdale Colliery in the Sirhowy Valley, Wales, still use canaries to detect any underground gas that could be fatal in the mines. The miners care for the birds but never name them for fear of becoming "attached." In a wonderful way the believer has One in his heart who bears witness of God's leading for us. We refer to the person of the Holy Spirit as the heavenly Dove. Our responsibility is to heed His warning call and thus we shall avoid quenching the Holy Spirit (1 Thessalonians 5:19).

Perhaps as you read this you feel psychologically defeated, physically ill or spiritually sick. The Holy Spirit is calling to you and wants to direct you to Jesus Christ who can make you a whole person. The Lord Jesus Christ, by the power of the Holy Spirit, wants to fight your battles, be your strength and wisdom, and your eternal friend (2

Timothy 4:17; Romans 8:35-39; Philippians 2:13).

The Lord's question must have surprised the man at the pool. He said, "Do you want to be healed?" (see John 5:6). This seems like a strange question, but Jesus Christ realized that there are many chronic invalids who have no hope of a cure. Others use their sickness as a means of getting sympathy and therefore do not want to be healed. The man's response to the question was that he lacked the means to be healed, but did expectantly await help.

The Lord's next words must have been even more surprising to the man for He told him to do three things—rise, take up his bed, and walk (John 5:8). Really the man was not capable of doing any one of these things, but he did them! He exerted himself in faith, risking failure in order to obey the Lord Jesus' command. The Lord Jesus met him at this point and the man was healed.

We need to expect opposition, for it tests our faith and strengthens us as we lean upon God.

God never asks us to do anything without giving us the power to obey. The obedience and the power are simultaneous. To refuse to obey in faith is to not experience the power. The Lord told the lame man to do the impossible! A lame man cannot stand up, but when Christ said, "Arise," the man stood. "Take up your bed," was the next command. This removed any possibility of relapse. The man rolled up his mat. Now, "Walk!" He did just that (John 5:9). Do you obey the Lord like that? Even if you do not see how you can do as He asks, do you obey Him? When the Lord tells you to do something, you can be sure He will give you the ability to do it!

The Lame Man Faces Opposition

The lame man immediately was faced with opposition in his life. This is inevitable for any Christian who is being obedient to the Lord. This man had chosen to begin a new life and had taken up his bed as the Lord Jesus Christ commanded. This symbolized Jesus saying, "Accept your circumstances and carry them in triumph in my power." The lame man walked out of his bondage to the place God called him to go, just as the new Christian walks from the bondage of the flesh into the realm of letting the Holy Spirit control his life and produce fruit (Galatians 5:19-25). "If we live in the Spirit, let us also walk in the Spirit" (Galatians 5:25).

Opposition is inevitable for an active Christian (1 Peter 2:20-21;

1 Thessalonians 3:3-4). We need to expect opposition, for it tests our faith and strengthens us as we lean upon God. God proves Himself as He comforts us in our trials. This lame man met the Jews and he began to get opposition (John 5:10-13). The people accused him of breaking the Sabbath by carrying his bed. This made him feel insecure because his knowledge of Jesus Christ was incomplete.

Often a new Christian feels insecure after he has come to the Lord Jesus Christ in faith, because he does not know all about Him. Yet we can learn from this story that step by step, just as the lame man moved forward, we as new Christians are to move forward in our knowledge of the Lord Jesus as we study His Word, the Bible. "But grow in grace, and in the knowledge of our Lord and Savior Jesus Christ. To Him be glory both now and forever. Amen" (2 Peter 3:18).

The question is how much time will you give the Lord in order to grow in grace and the knowledge of His Word? A survey in *U.S. News and World Report* shows that television ranks first—and organized religion eighteenth—among influences on daily living. One pastor is quoted as saying, "This beast that is among us [television] is perhaps the most important influence on our lives today."

Of course, not all programs have a bad influence and we must learn to be selective of what we watch as well as the amount of time we expend on television. Television is not the only thing that interferes with our time. Many other things entice us and lead us to become involved, such as activities and hobbies, so that we are kept from growing in our faith because we do not spend time each day reading the Bible and talking with God in prayer.

The first indication the Jewish people had of anything unusual was when they saw the man walking away from the pool, carrying the rolled up mat that he used for a bed. They did not rejoice that a man who had been unable to walk for 38 years was coming toward them! All they saw was one of their laws being broken (John 5:10). This was the beginning of the antagonism the Jews had toward the Lord Jesus. They were angry that their law had been broken, so angry that they sought the Lord Jesus to kill Him (John 5:18).

It is true that God had set the Sabbath day apart for rest for His people and a time to worship and show love to Him (Isaiah 58:13-14). In Exodus 20:8-11 the law said that no man, his servants, or his animals should do any work. This included such activities as trading or carrying heavy burdens for commercial purposes (Nehemiah 13:15-19; Jeremiah 17:19-27).

However, the Rabbis had carried the law to an extreme and said that a man was sinning if he carried a needle in his robe on the Sabbath, and they even argued about whether a man could wear artificial teeth or a wooden leg, or a woman wear a piece of jewelry on the

Sabbath. A man who spit on the ground on the Sabbath had to be careful that his spittle didn't roll in the dirt for it was considered "plowing a furrow!" This was illegal on the Sabbath.

The man's defense was that the one who had healed him told him to carry the pallet, and he eventually told them that this person was Jesus (John 5:15). The Lord Jesus deliberately chose the Sabbath day to perform many of His works of mercy. And this was one of the reasons the religious leaders hated Him and persecuted Him.

Before leaving this section we need to note that the Lord Jesus found this man in God's temple after he was healed, undoubtedly giving thanks to God for his strong legs and healthy body! When you receive the Lord Jesus Christ as your Savior and Lord, He wants to also find you in His Church praising Him with other Christians!

Jesus Claims to Be the Son of God
John 5:17-32

When the Jewish people found the Lord Jesus they forgot about the Sabbath problem for now He also claimed to be equal with God. "My Father worketh hitherto, and I work" (John 5:17). He wanted them to know that God is His Father and that He is God the Son. Over and over in the next few verses He uses the words "Father" and "Son."

The Jews were concerned with the idea of anyone working on the Sabbath. Jesus answered their concern. He taught that God did not stop working for the salvation of men. The Lord Jesus said, "My Father constantly does good, and I'm following his example" (John 5:17). The Jews recognized that His words were a direct condemnation of their lack of interest in the man who was healed, and their special interest in the keeping of their rules.

This One, standing before them, dared to put Himself on an equality with God. The Jews indicated that they did not believe Jesus had any right to make such a claim: The Lord Jesus said that He had every right (John 5:19-21). Notice the comparison between the Father and the Son. What the Father does, the Son does. What the Father sees, the Son sees. What the Father knows, the Son knows. The Father and the Son are equal. Jesus Christ is God!

Because the Son is equal to the Father, there are some things which are given to the Son to do. One of these is to judge men (John 5:22). The Lord Jesus Christ one day will judge all the people who ever lived. Those who have accepted Him as Savior will not come into this judgment, for their sins were judged when the Son of God shed His blood on the cross for them. Those who receive Him have everlasting life and will not be judged. The Lord Jesus Christ will be the judge of those who reject Him (John 5:24). Another power which

Jesus has because He is the Son of God, is the power to give life. He has the power to resurrect the dead. He has life in Himself (John 5:25-26; John 14:6).

Jesus makes a statement in John 5:30 which shows His submission to God the Father. "I seek not mine own will, but the will of the Father which hath sent me." Here is an example of total cooperation. The Lord Jesus did not seek His own will, but as perfect God and perfect Man He willingly gave Himself upon the cross so that anyone who comes to Him in faith might be forgiven his sins and in Him be given new life.

The Four Witnesses to the Lord Jesus Christ John 5:33-47

The Lord Jesus told the Jews that He spoke the truth. He told them that they should believe Him because of the proof He offered. First Jesus reminded the people of the witness of John the Baptist (John 5:32). John spoke of Jesus Christ, but the people would not believe his words. (See John 1:19-20,26,29,35,36.) The Lord Jesus then told these Jewish people that He did not depend only upon a mere human witness, but He was willing to use any witness they could understand.

The second witness was that Jesus had performed signs which showed His power; He had just healed a man who had been unable to walk for 38 years. Jesus said that they should believe Him for the works He did (John 5:36). Then He told the men that God the Father bore witness of Him (Matthew 3:17), but the people would not even believe the voice of God (John 5:37-38).

Finally the Lord Jesus said that the Scriptures bear witness of Him. The Jews read the Scriptures but they did not understand that He, Jesus Christ, was the One those Scriptures spoke of (John 5:39-47). The Pharisees who searched the Scriptures undoubtedly knew in detail all the prophesies concerning the Messiah, yet they refused to acknowledge that Jesus Christ was the Messiah.

To illustrate this, think of the Bible as a beautiful window overlooking a panoramic view of the countryside. Suppose that someone asked the owner to describe this window, and he said, "My window is made of glass and is eight feet long by five feet high. It is surrounded by a wood frame and is draped in red velvet. My window is one inch thick so that it keeps out the heat and the cold."

The owner would be missing the whole point, for this beautiful window was so he could enjoy the panoramic view of the valley below.

The Bible is a window through which we see Jesus Christ. The Pharisees had examined the Bible carefully and knew of its many details, yet they did not realize that the most important purpose for it was to point them to the Messiah, Jesus Christ. The Lord Jesus Christ tried to help them look through their Old Testament "window" with eyes of faith by saying in John 5:46, "For had ye believed Moses, ye would have believed me: for he wrote of me."

How sad to realize that there were so many evidences of the Lord Jesus Christ's deity and yet these men refused to receive Him and obey by responding in faith to Him. He told them how to have everlasting life (John 5:24) but they would not listen. They only sought to kill Him. He explained that He was God, but they would not worship Him. He said that the Scriptures told of Him, but they thought that by reading them they would have life.

Everlasting life is in Christ and only in Him. Do you have this everlasting life? Have you received this gift (Romans 6:23)? Have you passed from death into life (John 5:24)? If so, are you obedient to Him and cooperating with Him in sharing His life with others?

Study Questions

Before you begin your study this week:

1. Pray each day and ask God to speak to you through His Holy Spirit.
2. Use only your Bible to answer the following questions.
3. Write down your answers and, where called for, include the verses you used.
4. Challenge questions are for those who have the time and who wish to do them.
5. Personal questions are to be shared with your study group only if you wish to share.
6. As you study, look for a verse to memorize this week. Write it down, carry it with you, tack it to your bulletin board, tape it to the dashboard of your car. Make a real effort to learn the verse and its reference.

FIRST DAY: Read all of the preceding notes and look up all of the Scriptures given.

1. What was a helpful or new thought from the Overview of John 5?

2. What personal application did you select to apply to your own life?

SECOND DAY: Read all of John 6 concentrating on John 6:1-14.

1 a. Where did the Lord Jesus go after He left Jerusalem where the events of John 5 took place, and what two groups followed Jesus to this place?

b. When the Lord Jesus saw the crowd coming, what was His first thought? Give verse please.

c. Read John 6:3 and Mark 6:30-32. Why do you believe Jesus had gone to the mountain?

2 a. (Personal) What about you? What is your attitude toward someone who has a need? Do you feel antagonistic if your rest is interrupted? Do you have a carefully planned schedule for your minutes and determine to let nothing or no one interfere with your schedule?

b. According to the record of this story in Matthew 14:13-21 what did the Lord Jesus' disciples suggest He do with the crowd? Give verse please.

c. **Challenge:** Have you ever had the same reaction that the disciples had in Matthew 14:13-21 when someone came to you with great needs? How can the admonitions in 2 Timothy 2:3 and Philippians 2:5 and 2:13 encourage you to let Christ live in you and strengthen you in such a situation? Use your own wording if possible.

2 Timothy 2:3

Philippians 2:5,13

d. (Personal) Is there someone with a need in your neighborhood, office, or church? Will you trust God by writing in this space the concern that God has given you for them? Try to describe willingness to depend on Him to show you how to help this person or group.

3 a. How were Philip and Andrew honest in describing their doubts to the Lord Jesus? (See John 6:5-10.)

b. If you feel discouraged when someone comes to you for help, do you think it is a good idea to be honest like Andrew and Philip and take your attitudes and needs to the Lord Jesus in prayer? What does Philippians 4:6 tell the Christian to do? Put this into your own words if possible.

4 a. After reading John 6:10 and Luke 9:14-15, do you believe the Lord Jesus did things in an orderly way? Please give reasons for your answer.
   b. Do you believe more can be accomplished if you pray that the Lord Jesus will organize your day, moment by moment, to make it "orderly"? Share your examples; it may encourage someone else.

c. (Personal) Write down some of the specific areas which you want to ask the Lord Jesus to make "orderly" in your life. Then read Matthew 7:7-8 to encourage yourself concerning these prayer requests.

5. What did the Lord Jesus stop to do before He fed the crowd? Do you stop and do this, no matter where you are—at home or in a crowd?

6 a. Was there enough food? Was there any left over?

b. How did the Lord Jesus distribute the food to those who were seated? See Mark 6:41 for added details

c. (Personal) What particular thing do you think the Lord Jesus wants you to share with the crowds today? Read the following verses.

1 Peter 3:15

Colossians 3:16

THIRD DAY: Read John 6:15-21.

1. After the Lord Jesus fed the crowd what did they want to do to Him? What was His response to the crowd at this time?

2. **Challenge:** What was Christ's mission to people on earth at this time? Was it to be a king? What do the following verses say concerning this? Put them in your own words if you wish to.

Matthew 20:28

Luke 19:10

Luke 2:10-11

3. (Personal) By faith in Jesus Christ, can you write your name into 1 Timothy 1:15-16, thus making it your testimony of what Christ Jesus has done for you? Write it here.

4 a. What did the disciples do when evening came? See John 6:16-17.

   b. What happened after they had launched their boat and were on their way across the water?

5. What more do you learn about the stilling of the storm and walking on the water from Matthew 14:22-33? Give verses please.

6. (Personal) What favorite or challenging thought did you find for your life this week as you read Matthew 14:22-33?

FOURTH DAY: Read John 6:22-40.

1. Where did the crowd, whom the Lord Jesus fed, go to look for Him when they could not find Him on the mountain where He fed them? Try to find this place on your Bible map.

2. According to this passage why does the Lord Jesus say the crowd is following Him from place to place? Give verse.

3. What does the Lord Jesus say the crowd should be seeking?

4. What does Jesus call Himself in John 6:22-40? Give verse please.

5. What does Jesus say about the water that He will give to those who believe and receive Him in John 4:14?

6 a. (Personal) Do you have the Bread of Life and satisfying water in your life? Read Romans 3:22-28 to better help you know whether you have such joy in Jesus Christ.

b. Are you sharing the truths with others in your neighborhood, business and church? How are you sharing the "Bread of Life?"

FIFTH DAY: Read John 6:41-51.

1. Whom did the Jews believe the Lord Jesus' father was?

2. According to Matthew 1:18-22 and Luke 1:26-37 how was the Lord Jesus conceived and whose Son was He? Give verses.

3. What verses in John 6:41-51 speak of Jesus Christ being the Bread of Life and giving everlasting life?

4. (Personal) Which verse would you like to claim for your life today? Why? Which verse would you like to memorize to share with others? Why?

5. **Challenge:** Put John 6:51 into your own words as much as possible and put your name in place of "the world."

6. What does Acts 4:12 tell us about the Lord Jesus?

SIXTH DAY: Read John 6:52-71.

1. Where did the Lord Jesus teach that His flesh and His blood would bring eternal life to those who believed in Him?

2. How does Matthew 26:26-28 help you to understand better the Lord Jesus' words in John 6:52-58?

3. Challenge: How does 1 Peter 1:3 help you to better understand the words which the Lord Jesus spoke in John 6:52-58?

4. According to John 6:52-71 were all of those who followed Jesus Christ true believers in Him as the Son of God and Savior? Give verses.

5. What did Simon Peter say to the Lord Jesus which every true Christian should be able to whisper to the Lord in prayer also?

6. Which verse of Scripture in the study was most helpful to you this week? Do you choose to hide it in your heart by memorizing it?

JESUS OFFERS THE BREAD OF LIFE

John 6

Study Notes

The Feeding of the Five Thousand
John 6:1-14

Also recorded in Matthew 14:13-21, Mark 6:30-44 and Luke 9:10-17.

Jesus Christ spent most of His life in Galilee. He grew up in Nazareth, and much of His three years of ministry was in Galilee, with headquarters at Capernaum. John's record of the first year of Christ's ministry, closes with chapter 5.

Chapter 6 is the account of the events in the second year of the Lord's ministry. Possibly, John gave little space to the events of this period because the other three Gospels emphasized what the Lord did during this time. It is believed that these Gospels were already written and John undoubtedly read them and knew what the Holy Spirit had guided Matthew, Mark and Luke to write concerning the Lord Jesus Christ's life and ministry.

In John 6:2 we learn that a great multitude was following the Lord. From the other accounts of this event (Matthew 14:10-13) we learn that when Jesus heard about the death of John the Baptist, He went away to a desert place to be alone with His disciples. "And He said to them, 'Come away by yourselves to a lonely place and rest awhile.' For there were many people coming and going, and they had did not even have time to eat" (Mark 6:31). But the Lord did not receive any rest because the people saw Him leave and they followed Him.

The Importance of Quiet Time

In this Scripture Jesus also illustrates for us the necessity to "come away" by ourselves to be with Him, just as He tried to make time to be alone with His disciples of that day. As His present-day disciples, we need to spend time alone with the Lord Jesus, secluded from all of the pressures and busyness of our society. Do you manage to find some time during your day to have a quiet time alone with the Lord Jesus, listening to Him in your prayer time and as you read the Bible?

This study can help you develop the habit of disciplining yourself to make time to be alone with the Lord Jesus. Try to follow the study questions day-by-day this week, including the suggestion that you spend time in prayer before you go into your study. Perhaps you would like to begin a prayer notebook in which you record the date, your thanksgiving to the Lord, your requests and other things you want to talk about to the Lord. It is helpful to go back over this kind of prayer notebook and note the date when the Lord began to answer a request as well as each praise and thanksgiving item inscribed in your notebook. Buy a small spiral notebook and begin to record your prayer life.

Keeping a prayer record should not limit your prayer time. You can pray during each day as unceasingly as you breathe throughout the day. Often we make a note "pray for _____ at 2:00 P.M. Monday," only to find the slip on Tuesday. Obviously it completely slipped our mind. This is distressing.

Therefore, it is wise, if you are talking on the telephone or face-to-face with someone who asks for prayer, to say, "Let's pray about it right now." Then, pray right now! If you do not feel free to ask the person if you can pray aloud, sometimes your prayer can be spoken quietly, in your heart, while you listen to him talk.

The Lord Has Compassion

This time the Lord was not to have rest and a quiet time. The people followed. The disciples would have sent them away but Jesus had compassion for them. "First feed them," the Lord commanded (see Mark 6:34-37).

It was springtime. There was much grass (John 6:10), and probably many beautiful wild flowers in bloom. Can you imagine the peaceful view of the Sea of Galilee from this hill? What a lovely quiet place to rest! Yet the Lord Jesus had pity on the people who came rushing up the hill toward Him. There would be no rest.

What about you? What is your attitude toward someone who has a need? Do you feel antagonistic if your rest is interrupted? Do you have such a carefully planned schedule for every minute that you are determined to let nothing or no one interfere with it? When a person comes to you in need are you open to the Holy Spirit's leading? Do you have "pity and compassion" for him?

Giving Thanks for Food

In the record of John's Gospel we read that Jesus asked Philip a question. "Where are we to buy bread, that these [people] may eat?" (John 6:5). Why did the Lord ask him? To prove, to test or to examine him. The Lord gave Philip a chance to acknowledge that Jesus could do anything.

The Bible quickly informs us that Jesus did not ask Philip for advice, for the Lord Himself knew what He would do (John 6:6). Philip was a practical man; he looked around the desert (or deserted) place where they were. He did not see any place where food could be bought. Then as he thought of the problem, he realized that even if there was a place to buy the food, the disciples did not have the money to pay for it (John 6:7).

Andrew, Simon Peter's brother, had a suggestion, but it did not seem that it could be of much help! He noticed that there was a lad who had five barley loaves and two fish, and "What are they among so many?" he said (John 6:9). Everyone who stood near must have agreed that a little boy's lunch was not much help when there were 5,000 men beside the women and children (Matthew 14:21). There may have been as many as 15,000 who ate that day.

The Lord Jesus took the boy's lunch. Can you imagine the excitement of this little boy? It's a lovely day; people stream from Capernaum, Bethsaida and other towns to the west end of the lake.

What's up? Boys always want to go where the crowd is. This boy starts off with his lunch and, in boy fashion, probably stops along the way to eat from it. As he stands back in the crowd, Andrew comes and speaks to him. The boy looks shyly into his basket to see what is left. He counts, "Four, ah five crackers," and "one ah two sardines." Perhaps then the boy is brought to the front of the crowd by Andrew, and maybe the Lord places His hand upon his head as He gives the prayer of thanks (John 6:11).

Jesus always stopped and thanked His Father in heaven for the food: should we not also stop and thank our heavenly Father for our food before each meal? Whether we are alone, with our family, in a quiet place or in a public place, we need to remember that this food is a gift from God to us and we should thank Him for it!

A waitress was overheard to say, "I always know a Christian in the restaurant as I see him bow his head in prayer, and then I know a Christian as he complains about his food." Let us not be this kind of ambassador for the Lord Jesus. A pleasant word to encourage those who serve us is what pleases our Lord.

The Importance of Being Tactful

Many Christians need the gifts of grace, thoughtfulness and tact. The dictionary describes tact as: "to deal with others without giving offense." Jesus defines it as doing to others as we would have them do to us (Matthew 7:12). The word "tact" comes from the Latin word *tactus* which means "to touch." We must seek to touch the hearts of men—not knock them down with a club, or with bad manners. We must carefully weigh our words and habits. If we wish to influence people for the Lord Jesus, we must use our head as well as our heart!

A barber attended a meeting one night where the speaker stressed the need of witnessing for Christ "in season and out." He was convicted; so he determined that he would speak to the first customer who came into his shop. The next morning after the customer was seated and the apron tucked around his neck, the barber began vigorously to sharpen his razor. Then testing the edge, he turned to the man in the chair and asked, "Friend, are you ready to die?"

When the Lord intervenes, there is always more than enough. Jesus always satisfies our needs . . . look at the power of the Master.

The man looked at the razor and fled out the door—apron and all! The barber had shown zeal, but not wisdom, which the Holy Spirit could have given him. Today, ask God for that rare trait called "tact" in touching folks for Christ, whether it be in a restaurant, your business, neighborhood or home.

Give Your All to Christ

The Lord Jesus took the boy's lunch. As simply as John 6:11 puts it, Jesus created from the loaves and the fish enough food for all of the people, and when He told the disciples to gather up what was left, the fragments filled 12 baskets. This is the record of another sign of the deity of Christ.

When the Lord intervenes, there is always more than enough. Jesus always satisfies our needs. Let us not be like Philip who looked only at the few loaves and fishes. He forgot to look at the power of the Master.

Christ wants us to give to Him, in gladness, all that we have that

He might use it and increase it. If you want the Lord Jesus to bless your life, you must put everything in His hand, however small. Loaves unblessed by our Master, are loaves unmultiplied. No one else could have fed more than one with this skimpy lunch, but remember when you put your all—your best—freely, with love, in His blessed hand to use, He increases it.

If Christ tells you to speak a word for Him, do it. If Christ tells you to teach for Him, do it. His Holy Spirit will take your life, and work in you to bring someone to Jesus Christ. You will be blessed. Is not this your "reasonable service?" (Romans 12:1). Will you give the Lord Jesus Christ your abilities and talents as the boy gave the loaves and fishes to Him?

Jesus the "Rice/Bread" of Life

One day in south China an Oriental arose and addressed the missionary saying, "I have heard you speak three times, and you constantly have the same theme. Why don't you change it? You always speak of Jesus Christ."

The Christian replied, "Sir, before answering your question, may I ask you, 'What did you have for dinner today?'"

"Rice," replied the Oriental.

"What did you have yesterday?"

"The same thing."

"And what do you expect to eat in the future?" the Christian persisted.

"Rice, of course. It gives me strength. I could not do without it. Sir, it is . . . ," the Chinese gentleman hesitated as if looking for a strong word. Then he added, "Sir, it is my very life!"

The missionary responded quickly, "What you have said of rice, Jesus is to our soul! He is the 'rice' or 'bread of life.'"

Have you partaken of this wondrous Bread of Life? It can only be assimilated by faith. Only Jesus, the true Bread, can nourish starving souls.

Jesus Walks on the Water John 6:15-21

Found also in Matthew 14:22-32; Mark 6:45-52.

The Lord Jesus sent the disciples on ahead while He dismissed the crowds. Then He went up into the hills by Himself to pray (Matthew 14:22-23). However, Jesus did not forget the disciples, nor was He too busy with God to think about them. Even in His quiet time they were on His heart. Just so, the Lord Jesus watches out for you, and as a Christian you are just as dear to Him!

The disciples started to row across the Sea of Galilee toward Capernaum. A storm came up and it was night. Surprise winds typically sweep across the Sea of Galilee, even today, bringing unexpected storms. Jesus was not in the boat with the disciples, and they were frightened. Then, to add to their dismay, they saw a figure walking toward them across the water.

The Lord Jesus knew their fright and He called to them: "It is I; be not afraid!—I AM; stop being frightened" (John 6:20) "You need not be afraid; I AM!" That is what the Lord told the men.

If we know who Jesus Christ is, and that He is with us, we need not fear anything. This is another of the signs that John chose to show us that Jesus Christ is God. In many places in the Scriptures we find the Lord Jesus Christ referring to Himself as "I AM" (John 4:26, John 6:35, John 8:23,58, John 9:5, John 10:7, John 10:36, John 11:25, John 13:13, John 14:6, John 15:1, Revelation 1:8; Revelation 1:17).

When the Lord Jesus pulls you through the waves He holds you tight. He will not let you go.

This is the kind of story any fisherman would like to remember and would love to tell. Every time John thought about it he could feel that night again! The rough wind, the gray-silver of the moonlight on the lake, the flapping sail, the sound of the surging water and then the sudden unexpected appearance of Jesus Christ. Matthew 14:26 tells us that the disciples cried out, "It is a ghost," when they saw the figure walking on the sea toward them.

These men were battling the sea, rowing against a strong wind, trying to get to their destination. When they received the Lord Jesus into the ship, immediately they were at the land to which they were going.

When the Lord Jesus pulls you through the waves He holds you tight. He will not let you go (John 6:37).

The Living Bread John 6:22-59

The next day, perhaps around lunch time, some of the crowd of people were again at the place where Jesus had fed them. They knew that He had not gone with His disciples, and there was only one other small boat by the sea. Other small boats came from Tiberius but Jesus was not on them. So the crowd got into the boats and set off for Capernaum. There they found the Lord Jesus. He knew why they had followed Him.

The people spoke to the Lord Jesus as though they really wanted to do God's will. "What shall we do, that we may work the works of God?" (John 6:28). Jesus knew the people, and realized that they did not really believe in Him. He responded, "This is the work of God, that you believe in Him whom He has sent" (John 6:29).

The people could not please God nor do His work until they first learned to believe in Christ. They had to start with faith in Christ, then they could consider how to do good works to please God by the power of the Holy Spirit (see Zechariah 4:6; Romans 8:1,9-11; Philippians 2:13-16).

The people could not get their minds away from the free food (John 6:30,31). They wanted another miracle like the one they had seen the day before. They reminded Jesus that Moses had continued to feed the Israelites in the wilderness.

But they were wrong about one thing. Who did Jesus say gave the Israelites the manna that they ate? "My Father" (John 6:32). The people did not seem to care who gave them their bread, just so they got it (John 6:34). They had received one meal, now they wanted the promise of more in the future.

Then Jesus told the people how they could have the true bread from heaven, the Bread of Life. He said, "I am the bread of life. If you want to do the work of God, believe on me. If you want to receive the bread from heaven, you will have to come to me."

The people heard His words, but they did not believe in Him (John 6:36). The Lord Jesus Christ pointed out that anyone who comes to Christ will be received. He never turns His back on one who really seeks Him (John 6:37-40).

In John 6:49-51 Jesus repeats that He is "the bread from heaven, the bread of life, and the living bread." It is important that we know who Jesus is, but more important that we receive Him into our lives. To eat the Bread of Life means we believe in Jesus Christ (John 6:51). To drink of His blood (John 6:52-56) means we accept His death and resurrection for our sins. Remember, to believe is more than just to *know* something is true; to believe is to *act* upon what we know is true. (See Revelation 3:20.)

Homemade Bread

Do you remember coming home from school in the winter to a warm kitchen and seeing your mother take those first big brown loaves of homemade bread from the oven? She knew what you were waiting for, and would cut off a thick heel, plaster it with butter, and smile as you dug in! It was still hot and, oh, so good. You didn't have to disguise this bread with jelly, peanut butter or cheese!

What made this bread so much better? Was it because the loaves were twice as big as "store bread?" No, not that. The reason, was that it was not baked to sell for a profit, but it was prepared to please loved ones. Most of all, it was best because it was fresh, warm, soft and rich. It was homemade!

Jesus is the Bread of Life which we also must get firsthand. He is fresh, warm, soft and rich. To listen to a sermon or read a book about Him is "storebread." But if you want the best, then you must get it first hand from the Bible. Yes, Jesus, the Bread of Life, is most precious and sweet as you partake of Him directly from the Word of God. Nothing can substitute for this personal feeding upon Him!

Bread of God
train me not to
ruin my appetite
for You
by filling up on the goodies
and the trash
of this world.

—Nancy Spiegelberg

Eternal Life

When the people heard the words of the Lord Jesus in John 6:35-40 they turned away. "This is an hard saying," they said (John 6:60). They did not understand what He meant. The idea of eating His flesh and drinking His blood was not pleasant. In fact, it was forbidden to drink blood (Leviticus 17:10-14). The people did not understand Jesus' meaning nor did they want to believe.

"From that time many of His disciples went back, and walked no more with him"(John 6:66). The people heard what the Lord Jesus said. They heard that they would have eternal life if they believed in Him; that they would be resurrected if they followed Him (John 6:40). But they turned from Him!

In John 6:53 Jesus said, "Truly, truly, I say to you, unless you eat the flesh of the Son of Man and drink His blood, you have no life in yourselves. He who eats My flesh and drinks My blood has eternal life, and I will raise him up on the last day. For My flesh is true food, and My blood is true drink indeed. He who eats My flesh and drinks My blood abides in Me, and I in him."

The Lord Jesus used these terms metaphorically to illustrate a very important truth. For Him to shed His blood was necessary so that you might have everlasting life. His blood is life to the believer. To drink of His blood is to accept that Christ died for your sins. For life is in the blood (Leviticus 17:11). There is no remission (forgiveness) for your sins without the shedding of blood.

The writer of Hebrews 9:22 uses this same symbolism. "Without shedding of blood is no remission [of sin]." To "drink Christ's blood" means to believe that the Lord Jesus' blood was shed for the forgiveness of your sins, even if you were the only sinner in the world. The Lord Jesus Christ's flesh represents the life, "the Bread of Life," which God intended every person to have and is obtainable only by receiving the Lord Jesus Christ by faith.

The Holy Spirit enters you when you receive Jesus Christ by faith: "He who eats My flesh and drinks My blood abides in Me, and I in him" (John 6:56). Thus the eating of Christ's flesh is the positive act of faith in Him as Savior and Lord, and the dependence upon Him as you dwell in His Word, the Bible. Take His Word into your life. Act upon His promises believing that you will see the result of His promises because you are eating of the Lord Jesus Christ's "flesh."

Reread this passage of John 6 before taking Holy Communion in order to prepare your heart fully for the experience of the communion service. Other portions of Scripture which are very meaningful before Holy Communion are 1 Corinthians 11:17-34, Luke 22:7-30, Matthew 26:17-29, Mark 14:12-25.

Some Recognized Christ John 6:60-71

The Lord Jesus turned from the people to His disciples. "Will ye also go away?" He asked.

Peter spoke for the whole group: "There is no sense in going away; there is no one to whom we can go." Peter knew that Jesus had the way of eternal life. He is the only way to life (John 14:6). Peter spoke with assurance. Not only was there no one to whom they could go, but they did not want to leave the Lord Jesus.

Peter said, "We believe and are sure that thou art that Christ, the Son of the living God" (John 6:69). With these words that Peter declared comes another great conviction of who Jesus Christ really is. Jesus Christ really is the Son of God.

Where do you fit into the sixth chapter of John? Do you follow Christ like the crowd—for what you can get from Him? Many people want to make Christ a king because they think that He will give them an easy life.

Perhaps you feel like the crowd of people in the story that the Lord spoke a hard thing! Jesus Christ does make demands of His followers. Do not be like the crowd who turned away from Him! Follow Him closely. He does not say that it will always be easy, but He does say that it will be worthwhile.

113

Study Questions

Before you begin your study this week:
1. Pray each day and ask God to speak to you through His Holy Spirit.
2. Use only your Bible to answer the following questions.
3. Write down your answers and, where called for, include the verses you used.
4. Challenge questions are for those who have the time and who wish to do them.
5. Personal questions are to be shared with your study group only if you wish to share.
6. As you study, look for a verse to memorize this week. Write it down, carry it with you, tack it to your bulletin board, tape it to the dashboard of your car. Make a real effort to learn the verse and its reference.

FIRST DAY: Read all of the preceding notes and look up all of the Scriptures given.

1. What was a helpful or new thought from the Overview of John 6?

2. What personal application did you select to apply to your own life this week?

SECOND DAY: Read John 7 concentrating on John 7:1-9.

1 a. Why did the Lord Jesus stay in Galilee at this time?

   b. Find Judea (Jewry) and Galilee on your map.

2. **Challenge:** Compare the Lord Jesus' statement in John 7:6 with Matthew 26:17-19 and Matthew 27:26-50. What do you believe the Lord Jesus meant by "My time" in John 7:6 and Matthew 26:18?

3. What did the Lord Jesus' brothers want Him to do and why? See John 7:3,4.

4. What interesting statement does Jesus Christ make about His brethren or His brothers in Matthew 12:46-50?

5. What is the "Father's will" according to His Son, the Lord Jesus, in John 6:39,40?

6 a. (Personal) Have you ever, by a deliberate choice, believed in and received God's Son to be your Savior and Lord? If so, place your name in your Bible in the place of "everyone" and "him" in John 6:40—thus indicating your faith in these promises.

   b. According to John 6:39-40, what wonderful promises does the Lord Jesus make to the Christian?

THIRD DAY: Read John 7:10-24.

1. When did the Lord Jesus go to the Feast of the Tabernacles?

2 a. **Challenge:** What was the purpose of the Feast of Tabernacles which was celebrated each year in October by the Jewish people? Read Leviticus 23:39-44 which describes this feast as Moses told the children of Israel about it. Describe the feast briefly.

b. Do you have a similar type of day set apart in your culture? What should this day mean to a Christian?

3 a. What happened about midway through this Feast of Tabernacles? See John 7 and give the verse, please.

b. What caused the Jews to marvel at Jesus' teaching?

c. Where did Jesus say His doctrine or teaching came from?

4. For what reason did the Lord Jesus say the Jewish leaders were angry with Him?

5. What good advice did Jesus Christ give these men which could be very helpful to you in your life today? See John 7:24. Look at several translations of the Bible if possible to help you answer this question.

6. How could the following verses from the Scriptures help you as a Christian to be slow to judge and be careful to seek the Lord's wisdom in making a judgment of someone? Put these verses into your own words if you wish to.

Psalm 82:2-4

Proverbs 17:15;18:5

Proverbs 29:26

7 a. Which of the verses in question 6 would you find most applicable to our society?

   b. Which one would you like to choose to apply to your own life this week? How would you allow the Lord to work out His plan for wise judgment in your life today? Be specific. Share with your group if possible.

FOURTH DAY: Read John 7:25-36.

1. What were the people of Jerusalem saying about the Lord Jesus as He taught in the Temple?

2. What similar reaction to Jesus Christ do you read about in Matthew 13:54-58?

3 a. Read John 7:28,29 with John 6:38,39. Who was it that Christ was from? Who sent Him?

   b. Where did Jesus Christ ascend to, and where is He coming back to earth from according to Acts 1:9-11?

117

4. **Challenge:** Read Luke 21:27-36. What impresses you most about this passage concerning the return of Jesus Christ?

5. In John 7:30 we read that no man laid hands on Jesus for "His hour" had not come. Read Matthew 26:36-45 to discover what this "hour" would bring into Christ's life.

6 a. The Pharisees (the religious leaders) heard that many of the people believed in Jesus Christ because of His miracles. What was their reaction to this news? See John 7:32.

  b. What was the greatest sign yet to come which would show that Jesus Christ was God? He speaks of it in John 7:33,34,36.

  c. What wonderful words in John 14:1-11 did Jesus Christ speak about His return to heaven? How do they help you in your personal life? Try putting your name into each verse and claim their promises for your life.

FIFTH AND SIXTH DAYS: Read John 7:37-53.

1 a. If we are thirsty for the Lord, to whom are we to go? Give verse please.

b. What kind of water will a person receive who believes in Jesus Christ?

2. When Christ spoke of "living water" to whom was He referring?

3 a. What were the various opinions expressed about Jesus Christ at this time? Give verses.

b. (Personal) Which of these opinions do you choose to believe by faith?

4 a. **Challenge:** What do the following Scriptures say concerning the birth and lineage of Jesus Christ as the Messiah?

Jeremiah 23:5

Micah 5:2

Matthew 2:3-5

John 7:41,42

b. Where was the Lord Jesus Christ born? See Luke 2:1-7.

5 a. How did Nicodemus try to see to it that the Lord Jesus would get a fair hearing and judgment by the Pharisees? Give verse. See John 7:50 and following.

b. (Personal) Has there ever been a time when you should have taken the same stand for someone, just as Nicodemus did for the Lord Jesus?

c. (Personal) Is there some situation similar to this in your neighborhood, office or family where the love of Christ could be expressed through your fairness and open-mindedness in the situation? Will you trust Christ to help you in this situation?

d. What does Philippians 4:4-7 say to encourage you?

6. Which of the verses in this lesson were most helpful to you? Did you choose to memorize any of them so that you could recall them in time of need?

SATISFY YOUR SPIRITUAL THIRST

John 7

Study Notes

Jesus Delays His Arrival at the Feast
John 7:1-13

John 7 begins with the Feast of Tabernacles, an event which takes place in the fall, about October. In John 6, the time was Passover (John 6:4) which occurred in the spring of the year, about April. Most of the intervening time the Lord Jesus spent in Galilee.

"After this, Jesus went around in Galilee, purposely staying away from Judea because the Jews there were waiting to take his life" (John 7:1).

In John 6, Peter speaks for all of the Lord Jesus' disciples when he says, "Lord, to whom shall we go? thou hast the words of eternal life" (John 6:68).

Peter's confession is reinforced by the testimony of all of his disciples, "We believe and know that you are the Holy One of God" (John 6:69).

Yet within their ranks is treachery. Jesus foresees it and speaks of it, "'Have I not chosen you, the Twelve? Yet one of you is a devil!'" (He meant Judas, the son of Simon Iscariot, who, though one of the Twelve, was later to betray him) (John 6:70-71). Our Lord knew the source of this evil was the devil.

In Galilee the Lord Jesus withdrew for a time from the active opposition of the Judaean Jews. Their opposition resulted from the healing of the sick man (John 5:1-47). He then began to teach in Galilee (John 6:1), while awaiting the hour when He would become the Savior of the world (Matthew 26:17-19; Matthew 27:26-50).

When the Lord Jesus spoke about His "hour" and "time" He meant the time when He would give Himself up to be crucified for the sins of the world, including our sins. This was His mission when He

121

came to earth as a babe born in Bethlehem (Luke 2:1-7) and raised in Nazareth (Matthew 2:19-23). The Lord Jesus Christ was Perfect God—Perfect Man. "And this is the record, that God hath given to us eternal life, and this life is in his Son" (1 John 5:11). "She shall bring forth a son, and thou shalt call his name Jesus: for he shall save his people from their sins" (Matthew 1:21).

Paul, led by the Holy Spirit, wrote about God's wonderful forgiveness through the Lord Jesus Christ. As you read this Scripture put your name in each verse and claim these promises for yourself!

"Once you were under God's curse, doomed forever for your sins. You went along with the crowd and were just like all the others, full of sin, obeying Satan, the mighty prince of the power of the air, who is at work right now in the hearts of those who are against the Lord. All of us used to be just as they are, our lives expressing the evil within us, doing every wicked thing that our passions or our evil thoughts might lead us into. We started out bad, being born with evil natures, and we're under God's anger just like everyone else.

"But God is so rich in mercy; He loved us so much that even though we were spiritually dead and doomed by our sins, he gave us back our lives again when he raised Christ from the dead—only by his undeserved favor have we ever been saved . . .

"Because of his kindness you have been saved through trusting Christ. And even trusting is not of yourselves; it too is a gift from God. Salvation is not a reward for the good we have done, so none of us can take any credit for it" (Ephesians 2:1-5,8,9).

After you put your name in these verses and truly believe in Jesus Christ as your Lord and Savior, consider, how can you share this "good news" with others? There are many ways in which God can lead you to share the good news of Jesus Christ—teaching Sunday School in your church, leading or helping in a Bible study group, conversing with your business friends or neighbors and many other situations in which the Holy Spirit will lead you.

THE NEW GENERATION

Is it any wonder, Lord,
   that the new generation
      is rebelling against
         their parents' double standard
           of morals
              and their parents' worship of
                money and material things?

Most of them have never been shown

real love,
   real concern,
      real honesty,
         real morality,
            real worship of the true
               God, Jesus Christ, Lord and Savior.

Dear Lord, I pray that
   in their rebellion,
      in their struggle,
         in their search
            for real meaning in life,

May this new generation find
   by your Holy Spirit's leading,
      the Truth
         in Jesus Christ.

And Lord, somehow involve me
   in sharing YOU
      with this new generation.

—Doris Greig

"Jesus told him, 'I am the way—yes, and the Truth and the Life. No one can get to the Father except by means of me'" (John 14:6). "Yet faith comes from listening to this good news—the good news about Christ" (Romans 10:17).

The events of John 7 occurred during the Feast of Tabernacles. (See Leviticus 23:33-44.) This, the last of the annual feasts lasted for a week. The Feast of Tabernacles (or Booths), which took place in September or October, was the joyous thanksgiving for the ingathering of the harvest. The people lived in tents (tabernacles) for seven days during the feast to commemorate the 40 years the children of Israel lived in tents in the wilderness and depended entirely upon God for their food, water and protection.

Each day of the feast a procession of priests and Levites went to the Pool of Siloam and drew a pitcher full of water. They carried the water back to the Temple and poured it around the altar. This water was to remind the Jews of God's provision in the wilderness and of His promise of spiritual blessing to come.

On the last day of the Feast of Tabernacles this ceremony of pouring water over the altar of the Temple did not take place, for the wilderness Israelites arrived in their own land and no longer needed a miraculous provision of water. The future blessings had not yet come to Israel—so, no water was drawn on this day. This was the day that the Lord Jesus stood and proclaimed, "If anyone thirst, let him come to me and drink. He who believes in me, as the scripture has said, 'Out of his heart shall flow rivers of living water.' Now this he said about the Spirit, which those who believed in him were to receive; for as yet the Spirit had not been given, because Jesus was not yet glorified" (John 7:37-39).

As the time of the feast drew near, Jesus' brothers told Him that He should go to Jerusalem. They thought that in the capital city He might be able to do something spectacular. His half-brothers did not believe that Jesus Christ was the Son of God (John 7:3-5).

The Lord Jesus did not listen to His brothers. He did not come to earth to be made king! He had come to die (John 7:6-9; Matthew 26:17-19; Matthew 27:26-50). So the Lord Jesus stayed in Galilee and the brothers went to Jerusalem. Later, He went also, but not with the spectacular display as His brothers wanted, but "in private" (John 7:10). He knew that the Jewish people would be looking for Him at the feast and there would be conflicting thoughts between those who believed in Him and those who felt that He was leading the people astray (John 7:11-13).

Jesus Teaches in the Temple John 7:14-36

In the middle of the feast, Jesus went to the Temple and taught. The people were amazed at His knowledge and use of words. They were amazed and impressed when He fed them (John 6:1-14), now they were impressed with His grammar and knowledge. At the age of 12 the Lord Jesus had captivated the lettered and learned, both by His language and scholarship. This was when He appeared before the doctors in the Temple during a Passover feast (Luke 2:41-52)!

No wonder they asked, "How knowest this man letters, having never learned?" (John 7:15). If an uneducated man appeared among a crowd of lawyers and doctors and spoke with the choicest diction and with a profound comprehension, wouldn't everyone look at one another and say, "How can this be?" There must be a reason.

Christ gave the reason! As a youth Jesus told them, "I must be about my Father's business." This time He claimed, "The things that I say come from God" (see John 7:16). Those words would be impossible if they came from anyone else but the Son of God!

Jesus told the people that there was one way they could be sure His doctrine came from God. "If any of you really determines to do God's will, then you will certainly know whether my teaching is from God or is merely my own" (John 7:17). If they really wanted to know

124

the will of God, they would recognize that Jesus spoke the words of God. Anyone who wants to know the will of God must come to Jesus Christ, hear what He says, and believe Him.

Putting God to the Test

Some years ago a very popular teacher at Yale expressed atheistic ideas and an agnostic viewpoint to all of his students and fellow teachers. During a special series of meetings at the college a visiting preacher talked with the brilliant professor.

"Doctor," he said, "if the things that I have been preaching are true, and if Christ really forgives men who trust him, wouldn't you like to know and experience this reality and know the peace and joy it has given to so many Christians?"

After a thoughtful pause the professor answered, "Yes, I believe I would."

"Well, you can come to a certain knowledge of God if you will be sincere and honest with yourself and the Lord. Simply accept the challenge Christ offered in John 7:17, 'If any man will do his will, he shall know of the doctrine, whether it be of God.'"

The learned doctor said, "But I wouldn't know where to begin. I don't even know if there is such a Being as God."

> *When you believe on Jesus Christ, you do not have to depend upon a pitcher of water being brought to you, for you will have a river of living water flow from you. This is a real reason to rejoice!*

The preacher said, "Start like this—pray, 'Oh God, if there is such a Being—show me. I promise to follow such light wherever it leads.'" The minister told him that if he would do this he would find God!

Many years later the same professor of learning stood in the chapel before all the students of Yale and said, "I have long ridiculed preachers and churches, but I have made a discovery that they were in the light, and I was in the dark. I have put God to the test. I know that Christ is my Savior. By his grace [*G*od's *R*iches *A*t *C*hrist's *E*xpense] he shall be my friend and I will be his disciple forever!"

Here is an example when honest doubt, properly handled, became the vestibule of faith! I challenge any of you who doubt, either from an atheistic viewpoint of believing there is no God or an agnostic viewpoint of not being sure, to read a portion from the Gospels and from the Psalms each day for the next few weeks. Read with an open mind and a willing heart and see if God speaks to your heart!

Find God Now

Jesus went on to say that He would return to His Father (John 7:33-36). The Lord Jesus knew that the Jews were seeking to kill Him. But nothing they did could change God's plan. In verse 30 we read: "Then they sought to take him; but no man laid hands on him, because his hour was not yet come." Jesus told the Jews that He would be here a little while—they could do nothing to prevent it—then when His work was finished, He would return to His Father and they could do nothing to change this. (Matthew 26:36-45 describes "His hour" and Acts 1:9-11 describes His ascension into heaven and His promised coming again.)

The last words that the Lord Jesus spoke to the Jewish people at this time should have caused them to consider how important it was to listen to Him. "Ye shall seek me, and shall not find me," Jesus said (John 7:34). What a terrible thing—to seek the Lord Jesus and be unable to find Him. The Lord Jesus was warning the people that they should not turn away from Him; they needed Him. If they did not find Him, they could not come where He was (John 14:1-11).

The Last Day of the Feast John 7:37-53

One of the most dramatic acts of the Lord Jesus is described in this portion of John. For seven days the people had been living in booths, temporarily sheltered by the boughs of trees. Each day as the priest brought the water into the Temple, the people remembered how God had provided water for them in the wilderness.

On the eighth day of the feast the people gathered again in the Temple, but on this day there was no procession. The people rejoiced because this meant that their forefathers had arrived in the land after 40 years of wandering in the wilderness. That night all of the people would return to their homes either in Jerusalem or in the outlying areas of the land.

Jesus stood in the Temple on this last day. He saw the rejoicing of the people but knew that they were still in need of spiritual water. He knew they needed Him and the Holy Spirit who was soon to come. He had been the rock that brought forth water in the wilderness. "Our fathers . . . did all drink the same spiritual drink: for they drank of that spiritual Rock that followed them: and that Rock was Christ" (1 Corinthians 10:4, Exodus 17:6-7). Now He stood and cried, "If any man thirst, let him come unto me, and drink" (John 7:37). What an effect this must have had upon the people!

"He that believeth on me, as the Scripture hath said, out of his belly shall flow rivers of living water" (John 7:38). When you believe on Jesus Christ, you do not have to depend upon a pitcher of water being brought to you, for you will have a river of living water flow from you. This is a real reason to rejoice! This living water is the Holy Spirit (John 7:39) who, not only will satisfy you, He will become a source of life and blessing within you.

Thirst, Drink, Overflow

Do you see the pattern—thirst, drink, overflow (John 7:37-38)? This is always the spiritual sequence. We hunger and thirst for blessing; we come to Christ and are satisfied; and immediately, whether we realize it or not, there is an overflow to others. It is this overflow that results in outreach! Overflowing prayer that reaches beyond our self-ish circle, overflowing love, overflowing faith, overflowing giving, overflowing service are all workings of the Holy Spirit whom Jesus promised to every believer.

We hunger and thirst for blessing; we come to Christ and are satisfied; and immediately, whether we realize it or not, there is an overflow to others. It is this overflow that results in outreach!

Those who enjoy the indwelling Holy Spirit, a well of "living water," have a reservoir which can cause their lips to overflow with kind and gracious words of blessing. However, a Christian can allow his old nature to dominate him so much that the fountain of his speech brings forth both "sweet water and bitter" (James 3:10-11).

God Hears You

The apostle Paul realized how important it is for the Christian to control his tongue. In Colossians 4:6 we read, "Let your speech at all times be gracious (pleasant and winsome), seasoned [as it were] with salt, [so that you may never be at a loss] to know how you ought to answer any one [who puts a question to you]". Proverbs 10:11 says, "The mouth of a righteous man is a well of life"—that is, it should be a fresh flowing spring from the Holy Spirit, ever-pouring forth healing, help and encouraging words." What a rebuke this implies for those whose lips are inappropriately occupied with gossip, lies or obscenities.

One day there was a man at work handling baggage at a depot. As some of the baggage was very heavy and difficult to manage, he lost patience and began to curse.

A little girl watching him and hearing him, was shocked and frightened. Finally she said, "Oh, please don't talk like that! Don't you know that God hears you?"

The man was startled by her earnestness and her words of concern brought conviction to his heart. "Don't you know God hears you?" kept ringing in his ears. He was unable to rid himself of the sense of God's nearness which the little girl's question had given him. He went home in a sober and thoughtful mood. In fact, he seemed so unlike himself that his wife thought he was sick.

"No, I'm not ill," he told her, "but I'm thinking about something."

All that night the phrase, "God hears you" troubled him. It became the turning point in his life. Eventually the words that flowed from the lips of that little girl who knew the Lord did more for him than all the sermons that he had ever heard.

How different many conversations would be if we all remembered this story. How different our words would often be if we remembered "God hears you." There is a saying that goes like this, "The thoughts in the well of our heart are bound to come up in the bucket of our speech." Will you choose to let God deal with "the well of your heart" today, and let His Holy Spirit overflow in your heart and through your lips as you yield your heart and lips to the Lord Jesus Christ?

Nicodemus Defends Jesus

The people listened to the words of Christ. Some said, "This must be the prophet of whom Moses spoke" (see John 7:40, Deuteronomy 18:15,18). Others said, "No, I think this must be the Christ" (see John 7:41). Others argued that He could not be the Christ for He had come from Galilee. Yet, as we read the Scriptures we know they all confirmed that Christ was from Bethlehem as predicted in the Old Testament (Jeremiah 23:5, Micah 5:2, Matthew 2:3-5, Luke 2:1-7).

The Bible says, "There was a division among the people because of him" (John 7:43). We read in John 7:31 that many believed on Him, but they believed only that He was someone important. The leaders did not pay attention to the Lord Jesus or to His teachings.

Nicodemus said that the leaders should not judge Him without letting Him speak for Himself; but Nicodemus was soon quieted (John 7:50-52). Nicodemus, a member of the Sanhedrin, had secretly visited Christ (John 3:1-21). He knew that to seek to arrest Jesus was an illegal procedure (John 7:44) and he reminded them that they had not given Christ a fair hearing (John 7:51). Nicodemus was scornfully silenced with the charge that he, too, was acting like an ignorant Galilean and that no prophet had ever arisen out of Galilee (John 7:41,46,52).

What a sad picture! The Lord had taught—had proclaimed—that He would give living water to anyone who was thirsty. The only record we have of any results of what Jesus Christ said or did that day indicates that almost everyone rejected His offer of the living water, the Holy Spirit.

A. "If any man thirst, let him come unto me, and drink" (John 7:37). It is not a matter of how good we are or how bad we are; any person may come to the Lord Jesus. It is not a matter of "have you fasted and prayed?" but "any man"—any thirsty soul turning to the Lord Jesus in faith.

B. "Let him come unto Me." Christ gives each one a gracious invitation. He gave everything that you might have everything. He gave His life on the cross that you might have forgiveness and the Holy Spirit dwell within you. How many times we go to every other source except the Lord Jesus Christ.

C. "And drink." To drink and believe are the same. Do you believe that the Lord Jesus wants to satisfy you? How wonderful it is, then, that you want just what the Lord wants you to have.

Why does water flow from the taps in your house with such force? Because there is great pent-up power in the reservoirs that seeks outlet. So a living God yearns to fill you with His Holy Spirit, moment-by-moment each day.

It is important to know that the "living waters" flow from Christ, not from anyone else! He has an ever-fresh and ever-flowing fullness to satisfy all the spiritual thirsts of human souls. It is no mere trickle of a stream, but "rivers." It is not a static pool of dead water, but "living" waters, fresh, free, pure, life-bringing. What a lovely picture to the thirsty and drought-plagued. What a wonderful Savior and Satisfier!

D. The well of water in John 4:14 becomes a river. There is not only enough to satisfy your own life, but rivers of blessings shall flow out from you to others. You do your part by being obedient to God and He will do His part. Some are satisfied to be just a little channel of blessing, but God says if you drink of Him, His rivers shall flow through you—an Amazon or Mississippi of blessing! Christ can make you a blessing to others. Go to Christ, and His life within you in the person of the Holy Spirit will leave a trail of blessings like the stream in the wilderness that makes trees and grass to grow at the water's edge.

Make me a channel of blessing today,
Make me a channel of blessing I pray;
My life possessing.
My service blessing,
Make me a channel of blessing today.

129

Study Questions

Before you begin your study this week:

1. Pray each day and ask God to speak to you through His Holy Spirit.
2. Use only your Bible to answer the following questions.
3. Write down your answers and, where called for, include the verses you used.
4. Challenge questions are for those who have the time and who wish to do them.
5. Personal questions are to be shared with your study group only if you wish to share.
6. As you study, look for a verse to memorize this week. Write it down, carry it with you, tack it to your bulletin board, tape it to the dashboard of your car. Make a real effort to learn the verse and its reference.

FIRST DAY: Read all of the preceding notes and look up all of the Scriptures given.

1. What was a helpful or new thought from the overview of John 7?

2. What personal application did you select to apply to your own life this week?

SECOND AND THIRD DAYS: Read John 8 concentrating on John 8:1-11.

1. After Jesus taught in the Temple on the last day of the feast (John 7:37-52), where did He go to spend the night? Give verse please.

2 a. Where did the Lord Jesus return to and at what time of day? What did He do in this place?

b. (Personal) If possible, do you choose to meet with the Lord early in the morning for prayer and Bible study? The Lord Jesus teaches us each day through this. If you cannot meet with Him for an extended time early in the morning, do you take the time to greet Him when you wake and talk with Him: thanking Him for the new day and for other blessings and asking for His guidance and strength for your day?

3. **Challenge:** What do the following verses say concerning prayer? Put them into your own words if you wish.

Psalm 118:5

Psalm 50:14-15

4 a. Whom did the scribes and Pharisees bring to the Lord Jesus? What kind of person was this? See John 8:1-3.

b. What did the scribes and Pharisees say that Moses' law said about such a woman?

c. What was Jesus' response to their questioning?

d. What happened to the Jewish scribes and Pharisees after Jesus said this?

5. How does John 8:7-9 confirm what Romans 3:23 states about all mankind?

6 a. After the Lord Jesus forgave the woman her sin, what did He say to her in John 8:11?

   b. **Challenge:** How does Romans 6:11-14 add to the words of Jesus Christ in John 8:11? Put these thoughts into your own words if you wish to.

FOURTH DAY: Read John 8:12-20.

1 a. As the people whom Jesus Christ had been teaching in the Temple watched all of this dialogue between the Lord Jesus and the scribes, Pharisees and the woman, they must have been amazed! What did He say to these people in the Temple in John 8:12?

   b. What does John 1:4 say to add to the truth which the Lord Jesus presented to the people in the Temple?

2. **Challenge:** Darkness represents sin, and light represents the Lord Jesus Christ. What, in your own words, do these verses say concerning the light who is Jesus Christ?

   Psalm 27:1

   1 John 1:5

   Revelation 21:23

132

3 a. In John 8:14-16 how did the Lord Jesus describe the way in which the Pharisees were judging Him?

   b. How did He describe His judgment in John 8:16-18?

4 a. What does 1 Samuel 16:6-7 say is the difference between man's judgment and God's judgment?

   b. (Personal) What can you learn about judgment from John 8:14-18 and 1 Samuel 16:6-7? Share if possible.

5. Read John 8:18-20. What question did the Pharisees ask the Lord Jesus and what was His response to it?

6 a. Where did Jesus speak all of these words?

   b. Why was it that no one arrested Him for making the bold statement that God was His Father?

   c. **Challenge:** How do Mark 8:31 and John 7:33 help you to understand "his hour" in John 8:20?

FIFTH DAY: Read John 8:21-30.

1. **Challenge:** How does John 14:6 help you to understand John 8:21? Note that the Lord Jesus knew these men's hearts and saw their sin of unbelief as He spoke these words to them in John 8:21.

2. How does the Lord Jesus contrast the people He spoke to and Himself in John 8:23?

3. Underline the following words in John 8:24, "for if you believe not that I am he, ye shall die in your sins." Also underline John 8:58. Note "I am" is in both verses.

4. How does God identify Himself in the following verses?

   Exodus 3:14

   Deuteronomy 32:39

   Isaiah 43:10

   Revelation 22:13

5. **Challenge:** What do you believe "lifted up" means in John 8:28? See John 12:32 and Luke 9:22 to help you understand and explain the Lord Jesus' statement here.

6 a. Whose will did the Lord Jesus seek to do and whom did He always seek to please? See John 8:28,29.

b. Who was always with the Lord Jesus to help Him? Give verse.

c. (Personal) Do you seek to be like the Lord Jesus as question 6a describes Him? How can this be possible? See James 4:13-15 and Matthew 28:18-20.

SIXTH DAY: Read John 8:31-59.

1. Compare 2 John 1:9 with the Lord Jesus' words in John 8:31.

2. **Challenge:** What do you believe the Lord Jesus meant by His statement in John 8:32? See Romans 8:1-5 to help you with your answer.

3 a. (Personal) Have you been freed from being a slave to sin (John 8:34) and do you set your mind and heart on the things in which the Holy Spirit leads you? See Romans 8:5.

b. What does Romans 8:6 promise you when you put your trust in God's Son Jesus Christ and set your mind on the Holy Spirit?

4. What did the Lord Jesus say about those who refused to believe that He is God, sent to earth by God the Father? Give verse in John.

5 a. Find all of the statements in John 8 that the Lord Jesus makes about the devil and give a verse reference for each statement, please.

   b. Who does the Lord Jesus say tells the truth?

6 a. What is the Lord Jesus' answer when He is asked by these men who He claims to be? See John 8:54-55.

   b. What was the reaction of Jewish men to this statement of Jesus?

   c. Look at Jesus' statement in John 8:55—"I keep his word." What word of the Lord would you like to keep this week by memorizing it? Choose a verse from the Bible and see if you can "hide it" in your heart and keep it there this week. Share it with your discussion group if possible.

THE LIGHT OF THE WORLD

John 8

Study Notes

The Lord Jesus Teaches in the Temple
John 8:1-11

If you knew that you had only a year to live, what would you do in that year? The feeding of the 5,000 occurred at the time of the Passover (John 6:4), just a year before our Lord's crucifixion.

In the seventh chapter of John we have the record of the Feast of Tabernacles which occurs in the fall of the year about six months after Passover and the feeding of the 5,000. John leaves out the events of the six months between Passover and the Feast of Tabernacles, except for the Transfiguration. The first nine chapters of Mark and Luke record other events during this six-month period. The discourse in the eighth chapter of John probably followed immediately the Feast of Tabernacles. We are about to discover what the Lord Jesus chose to do in the last six months of His life.

John 7:53 says, "And every man went unto his own house," and then in John 8:1 we see the Lord Jesus Christ, in His loneliness, as He goes to the Mount of Olives. Jesus had said, "Foxes have holes, and the birds of the air have nests; but the Son of man hath not where to lay his head" (Matthew 8:20).

I wonder, as the Lord Jesus spent that night on the Mount of Olives how He felt knowing that this would be the place where He would stand in about six months when His hour would come, and He would ascend into heaven to His Father. It would appear that Jesus

137

Christ spent that night, lying against some fallen tree or rock, alone with God. Meanwhile those who went to their houses, according to the Gospel of Matthew, held a counsel against Him and plotted how they might destroy Him.

Imagine the scene in John 8 as a committee meets to seek a means to destroy Jesus Christ. The "Get Jesus Committee" had the idea to first go right out in the public and ask Him if He paid His taxes. If He said, "Yes," they would tell the Jews, "Look, He says to support Caesar. What kind of a Messiah is this?" If He said, "No," the committee would say to Caesar's men, "We're very sorry, but Jesus is advising the people that they shouldn't support the government, and we want to be loyal to the Romans. You'd better arrest Him, and deal with Him."

In Matthew 22:16-22 we read of the actual carrying out of this plan. The next day they went to the Lord Jesus and said, "Master, is it lawful to give tribute unto Caesar?"

And He said, "Show me the money for the tax. Whose image is on the coin?"

"Caesar's."

"Well," said, Jesus, "if you're going to accept the protection of the Roman government—their fire department, their police, their army—then you've got to pay the freight on it! Render unto Caesar the things that are Caesar's, and render unto God the things that are God's."

At the next committee meeting they said, "Well, that one blew up in our faces. Now what can we do?"

And they kept at it, time and time again, testing the Lord Jesus to prove Him, to try Him, to catch Him. For they hated Him.

Putting an Old Law to the Test

Then John records one of the most despicable things that human beings have ever done. They remembered the old law from way back in the time of Moses that said that anyone caught in the act of adultery should be stoned to death. That law had not been put into practice for generations in their land. Just as today, men pass laws that become obsolete after a few years, but they fail to remove them from the law books.

For example, in the state of Delaware there is a law that says anybody approaching an intersection in a horseless carriage must come to a full stop, get out, and go to the intersection, by day with a red flag, and by night with a red lantern. You must be very careful not to scare the horses! That law was passed in 1902 and never taken off the books. But no policeman will ever arrest you if you don't have a red flag and a red lantern in your automobile as you go through Wilmington, Delaware!

This law from the time of Moses that anyone taken in adultery should be stoned to death, was God's law, but little by little, because of the hardness of men's hearts, it had been allowed to go unnoticed. In fact, it probably had not been enforced for the last 1,000 years before Christ. Yet one of these men had studied law and knew about it. So the committee decided, "Suppose we get a woman in the act of adultery." One wonders where they found this woman! Someone knew where to go! Certainly at least one of them had the right information because they were able, with just a few hours' notice, to find just the person they wanted.

Early the next morning, Jesus was sitting in the Temple teaching the people who had come to Him. Today, in Arab mosques, teachers still sit on the floor with their listeners as they teach. This position for teaching is still practiced in some of the synagogues of the Jews also.

The Lord Jesus was sitting in the Temple teaching. No doubt everyone was sitting quietly listening to Him. Then suddenly there was noise, angry voices, shouts, perhaps a woman's loud voice and into the study group came a crowd of men dragging an angry woman. They brought her through the crowd surrounding Jesus. They threw her on the ground and stood defiantly before Jesus (John 8:3). They brought this woman not because they hated adultery, nor because they wanted to uphold Moses' law; not even because they loved righteousness! They brought her because they hated Jesus Christ. They stooped so low that they took a poor woman and used her as a club to strike at Christ.

After demanding that the adulterous woman be stoned according to the law of Moses, the men asked Jesus what He had to say in response to their demands (see John 8:5). Did their question present a problem? Yes, but wait! The Jews were not allowed to execute a person. Only the Romans could. Thus, if Jesus were to say, "Kill her," the Roman authorities would oppose Him. If He were to say, "Free her," He would be opposing the law of Moses.

So, we see the problem. Perhaps these men planned to shout, "Oh, he's breaking the law of Moses! He tells us not to keep the law right in the Temple of God. We must be faithful to God and kill Him." They thought they had Jesus trapped. They might even have carried stones with them, hoping that they could kill Him right in the Temple!

What would you have done in such a situation? The Lord Jesus knew just what to do. He ignored the men. He stooped down and with His finger, wrote on the ground as though He had not even heard them (John 8:6).

139

The Hand Writing of God

Three incidents are recorded in the Scriptures when the finger or hand of God wrote something:

First, God gave Moses the Ten Commandments on two tablets of stone, that were written by His finger (Exodus 31:18).

Again, during a feast given by King Belshazzar, the finger of God in the form of a man's hand wrote on the wall, *Mene, Mene, Tekel, Parsin* which interpreted meant, "You have been weighed in the balances and have been found deficient." In other words, "You have been judged!" (See Daniel 5, particularly 5:24-28.)

Now, the third time in the Scriptures when the finger of God wrote is this incident in John 8:6. It is as though Jesus were saying, "Will *you* remind *me* of the law? I wrote the law." (See John 1:1,2.)

Jesus is God. It was He who gave the Ten Commandments. What did Jesus write on the ground? Perhaps it was "Thou shalt not commit adultery" (Exodus 20:14) or "The wages of sin is death" (Romans 6:23). The Bible does not tell us what He wrote.

Jesus, the Master Negotiator

However, the Jews continued to ask Jesus what punishment this woman should have. So He said, "He that is without sin among you, let him first cast a stone at her" (John 8:7)

Jesus gave the problem back to her accusers. All who had heard it, being convicted by their own conscience, went out one by one beginning with the oldest, who had the most sins to remember, to the youngest, who hadn't even lived yet. (See John 8:9.)

Jesus reminded them that they had all sinned and reminds us that we have all sinned too (Romans 3:23). Those who had come to trap the Lord Jesus sneaked quietly away into the crowd. They had come to condemn, but went away condemned themselves.

What happened to the woman? The Lord Jesus turned to her and said, "Woman, where are those thine accusers? hath no man condemned thee?" (John 8:10). The woman replied that no man had condemned her. Jesus said, "Neither do I condemn thee: go, and sin no more" (John 8:11).

Notice that the Pharisees called Jesus "Master," but this woman called Him "Lord." First Corinthians 12:3 says, "No one can say, ' Jesus is Lord,' except by the Holy Spirit." The Pharisees, if they did not change their attitude after that day, are in hell. The woman is in heaven. She has been forgiven by the Lord Jesus, and told to go and sin no more (see Ephesians 2:8-9).

When Jesus said, "Neither do I condemn thee: go and sin no

more," He was not condoning adultery, nor was He making a detour around the law. In the statement, "Neither do I condemn thee" is God's forgiveness and salvation; in the statement "Go, and sin no more" is God's sanctification (1 Thessalonians 5:23).

Jesus Is the Light of the World John 8:12-20

Jesus then turned to the people who had gathered in the treasury of the temple (John 8:20), located in the Court of Women. Giant oil-burning candelabras or Menorahs had been placed in the treasury for the Feast of the Tabernacles. These lights reminded the people of the pillar of fire that God sent to guide their ancestors through the wilderness (Exodus 40:38).

The light of life is available to all who follow the light of the world—the Lord Jesus Christ.

Every evening during the feast, the light from the candelabras shone over the city. Now the lights were out. The feast was over. Jesus looked at these darkened lamps and announced, "I am the light of the world" (John 8:12). Similarly, Paul writes of God's people "drinking from a spiritual rock" and "the rock was Christ" (1 Corinthians 10:4). Jesus then is both the Rock from which we receive water and the pillar from which we gain light. The water which Jesus gives is "living water" (John 7:38,39). And the light which He gives is the "light of life" (John 8:12).

The light of life is available to all who follow the light of the world—the Lord Jesus Christ. Jesus said, "He that followeth me shall not walk in darkness" (John 8:12). Darkness represents sin and death, but in Jesus Christ is life, "and the life was the light of men" (John 1:4).

"The Lord is my light and my salvation; whom shall I fear? The Lord is the stronghold of my life; of whom shall I be afraid?" (Psalm 27:1). "This is the message God has given us to pass on to you: that God is light and in him is no darkness at all" (1 John 1:5). (See also Revelation 21:23; Revelation 22:3-5.)

The verbal argument between the Jewish men and Jesus Christ continued. These men were doing their best to prove Jesus wrong or to catch Him in an inconsistency. They questioned His witness concerning Himself (John 8:13). They challenged His right to judge (John 8:16).

Each time Jesus Christ claimed that God was His Father, that His

141

and His Father's judgment was true and they judged together (John 8:16). "I can do nothing on my own authority; as I hear, I judge; and my judgment is just, because I seek not my own will but the will of him who sent me" (John 5:30).

Again Jesus claimed that God was His Father (John 8:18,19). This time the Jewish leaders did not question what He said; they became sarcastic. "Where is thy Father?" (John 8:19) they asked. In other words, "Produce God if you can," they seemed to say.

Jesus replied, "If ye had known me, ye should have known my Father also" (John 8:19). Most of these poor men were never to know the Lord Jesus Christ as God, nor would they know His Father. They were like the clumsy, finless tadpoles which scurry about in the ponds in August. These brown, speckled and black pollywogs have a tiny mouth; but the rest of their anatomy is stomach and a poor excuse for a tail. If they are kept in fresh water, in sunlight, eventually they will become adult frogs, like their parents.

However, if they remain in the dark, they will never develop front and hind legs like a frog, but will grow up to be big, fat tadpoles. To develop limbs that will enable them to jump or climb out of the pool slime, they need sunlight. Without that light they are destined to die in the mud.

A parable is hidden in all of this. Man, too, is born in darkness. Education, culture, science, philosophy and other human endeavors may enlarge the intellect and cause men to become great world figures, but without Christ they will live and die in the muddy pond of sin (Romans 3:23). Only through the Lord Jesus Christ who is the light of the world, can the poor, condemned sinner be delivered from the darkness of eternal death (Romans 6:23).

Jesus is the life and the light. Have you received Him today as your personal Savior and Lord? Are you sharing the life and the light of the Lord Jesus Christ with others?

Jesus Warns Against Unbelief John 8:21-30

The Lord Jesus Christ told these people He would go away when His hour came (Luke 9:22, John 12:32). He said, "I go away, and you shall seek Me, and shall die in your sin; where I am going, you cannot come" (John 8:21). He spoke these words to those who would not believe Him. In John 8:24 He pointed out that there was still opportunity to believe Him.

The Lord Jesus did nothing on His own authority, but only what the Father had taught Him to do (John 8:28). He was doing the will of His Father in heaven (John 4:34 and 5:19,20; John 6:38). Some of His hearers believed the words of Jesus (John 8:30), but He knew that their belief was shallow. So He said, "Continue in my word," continue to believe (John 8:31).

Do you seek to be like the Lord Jesus and to do the will of God? The Lord Jesus wants us to do what is pleasing in God's sight. "How do you know what is going to happen tomorrow? For the length of your lives is as uncertain as the morning fog—now you see it; soon it is gone. What you ought to say is, 'If the Lord wants us to, we shall live and do this or that.' Otherwise, you will be bragging about your own plans and such self-confidence never pleases God" (James 4:14-16).

Are these words from James meaningful in your life? Would you like to make them a prayer for your life-style and let the Lord guide you moment by moment through your days? Why not stop and ask God to make this Scripture come alive in your life right now? Why not yield your life fully to God's plan?

Think for a moment what motivates your service. Some Christians serve as if they were slaves, under fear. This is no motive! Others act as hired hands earning their wages—under the same principle of fear. We cannot earn salvation. "For by grace you have been saved through faith; and this is not your own doing, it is the gift of God—not because of works, lest any man should boast" (Ephesians 2:8-9).

What God really desires is that we perform deeds, serve just to please the Father, out of our love for Him. Only through this attitude can our lives and service bring blessing to others and praise to the Father. There is an old saying which is very true—"True service is love in working clothes." What kind of service have you been giving the Lord?

The True Children of Abraham John 8:31-59

"If ye continue in my word . . . the truth shall make you free," Jesus said (John 8:31,32). The Jews did not understand these words because they did not realize that they were not free. They were in bondage to sin. There is only one way to be free from sin—and that is through Christ (John 8:36).

Some Jewish people declared, "Abraham is our father," (John 8:39) so Jesus told them that if they were truly Abraham's children, they would do what Abraham did. "Thus Abraham 'believed God, and it was reckoned to him as righteousness.' So you see that it is men of faith who are the sons of Abraham. And the Scripture, foreseeing that God would justify the Gentiles by faith, preached the gospel beforehand to Abraham, saying, 'In thee shall all the nations be blessed.' So then, those who are men of faith are blessed with Abraham who had faith" (Galatians 3:6-9).

143

Romans 4:2,3 gives us further insight into Abraham's faith, "For if Abraham was justified by works, he has something to boast about, but not before God. For what does the scripture say? 'Abraham believed God, and it was reckoned to him as righteousness.'"

Often people still think like these Jewish men did in Jesus' day. They believe that they are already free. They are afraid that if they come to Christ and yield themselves to Him, they will forfeit their freedom. Nothing is further from the truth.

"For all who rely on works of the law are under a curse; for it is

Sin is like a disease; unless arrested, it progressively becomes more serious and more extensive.

written, 'Cursed be every one who does not abide by all things written in the book of the law, and do them.' Now it is evident that no man is justified before God by the law; for 'He who through faith is righteous shall live'; but the law does not rest on faith, for 'He who does them shall live by them.' Christ redeemed us from the curse of the law, having become a curse for us—for it is written, 'Cursed be every one who hangs on a tree'—that in Christ Jesus the blessing of Abraham might come upon the Gentiles, that we might receive the promise of the Spirit through faith" (Galatians 3:10-14).

Choosing Freedom

Think about a problem like this: a train is traveling down the track. It goes fast and safely as long as it stays on the track. But suppose the train gets the idea that it wants more freedom. It says to itself, "I would like to cut across that field and run along beside that stream."

So the train jumps the track. Instantly it lands in a ditch. It cannot go anywhere until somehow it is put back on the track. So it is with us. We cannot go anywhere until we are on the "track" that God's will and love have laid down. And on this track we have freedom.

A famous blacksmith of medieval times committed a crime for which he was put into a dungeon and chained to the wall. He began to examine the chains to see if he could discover some imperfection that might make it easier for him to break the chain. After a few minutes he groaned, "Oh, God, help me! I am bound with a chain that *I* made! I can never break it."

The Jews in Jesus' day were in bondage, chained by sin that they themselves had made. Everyone who does not know Jesus Christ is bound by the chains of his own sin. Jesus said, "Whosoever committeth sin is the servant of sin" (John 8:34). How can we be freed from the bondage of sin? The blacksmith was right; we cannot break the chains ourselves.

A prisoner did not like to see the bars on the window of his cell; so he trained ivy to grow around them. After several years the bars were covered. The poor man felt better because he could not see the bars, but the bars were still there! Many people today are ignoring or covering over the bondage of sin and really believe that this will be the answer to their problem. But the bondage of sin will not be broken by ignoring it! There is only one way. Underline John 8:36 in your Bible, "So if the Son makes you free, you will be free indeed."

Trust in God

The Lord Jesus declared in John 8:45-47 that He is telling the truth to these people and asks why they will not believe Him? He tells them the reason they will not believe Him is because they do not trust in God. In John 8:51 we find a significant statement by Jesus Christ— "Truly, truly, I say to you, if any one keeps my word, he will never see death." Everyone has sin, all of us have willfully broken God's commandments. Sin is like a disease; unless arrested, it progressively becomes more serious and more extensive. Just as a sick person is held captive by his disease, so every sinner is a slave of his sin.

Thank God this is not the only picture. We can have our sins forgiven. We can receive eternal life from the Lord Jesus Christ. We can know where we are going. We can be secure in the knowledge that in following Christ we do not walk in darkness, but we are in the light of life (John 8:12). We can be free from the bondage of our sin because Christ breaks the chains and gives us freedom (John 8:36).

In John 8 there are several names and titles given to the Lord Jesus Christ. "Jesus" is one of them. "Jesus" means Savior (Matthew 1:21). Is He your Savior?

Jesus is also called "Master," which means teacher. Is He your teacher? Jesus said, "If any one keeps my word, he will never taste death" (John 8:52). Are you allowing the Lord Jesus Christ to teach you from His Word, the Bible?

The Lord Jesus is also called "Son" (John 8:28). Do you worship Him as the Son of God? Is He your "Lord" (John 8:11)? Does He guide you as the "Light of the world" (John 8:12)?

Study Questions

Before you begin your study this week:

1. Pray each day and ask God to speak to you through His Holy Spirit.
2. Use only your Bible to answer the following questions.
3. Write down your answers and, where called for, include the verses you used.
4. Challenge questions are for those who have the time and who wish to do them.
5. Personal questions are to be shared with your study group only if you wish to share.
6. As you study, look for a verse to memorize this week. Write it down, carry it with you, tack it to your bulletin board, tape it to the dashboard of your car. Make a real effort to learn the verse and its reference.

FIRST DAY: Read all of the preceding notes and look up all of the Scriptures given.

1. What was a helpful or new thought from the overview of John 8?

2. What personal application did you select to apply to your own life this week?

SECOND DAY: Read John 8:51-59.

1 a. Whom did Jesus Christ say glorifies Him?

b. Whom did Jesus Christ say did not know God the Father?

2 a. What did the Lord Jesus say about Abraham in John 8:56?

   b. What was the Jewish men's response to this statement of the
      Lord Jesus?

3. Read Hebrews 11:8-16 and write down Hebrews 11:13.

4. What did the Lord Jesus say about Himself in John 8:58?

5. Jesus Christ calls Himself "I AM" in John 8:58. Read Exodus 3:1-
   15. What does God tell Moses about "I AM"?

6 a. **Challenge:** Jesus Christ also identifies Himself as "I AM" and
     makes Himself equal with God in other passages. Find His
     statements about being "I AM" in the following verses.

     John 10:7-11

     John 11:25

     John 14:6

     John 15:1,5

John 8:12

Revelation 1:8

b. Which of the verses in question 6a is your favorite? Share why it is your favorite verse.

THIRD DAY: Read all of John 9 concentrating on John 9:1-12.

1 a. Whom did Jesus Christ see?

   b. What did His disciples ask about him?

2. What did the Lord Jesus reply to this question?

3. What did the Lord Jesus say concerning Himself in John 9:5?

4. What did the Lord Jesus do for this blind man? See John 9:6-7.

5. Was the blind man obedient to the Lord Jesus' words and what blessing did he receive from Him for obeying in faith?

6 a. **Challenge:** What do the following verses say concerning obedience to God? Put them into your own words if you wish to.

Exodus 19:5

Psalm 119:2

Psalm 143:10

Matthew 6:24

Acts 5:29

b. Which of these verses was most meaningful to you? Explain why, and share this thought with someone if possible.

FOURTH DAY: Read John 9:13-23.

1. What day was it that Jesus Christ made the clay and opened the man's eyes?

2. What did the Pharisees say about the Lord Jesus? Tell why. See John 9:16.

3. **Challenge:** What do the following verses say about the Lord Jesus Christ and sin? Put them into your own words if you wish.

   2 Corinthians 5:20-21

1 Peter 2:22

1 John 3:5

Isaiah 53:5-6

4. What did the man, whose sight had been restored, call the Lord Jesus in John 9:17?

5. Why were the blind man's parents afraid to make any statements about the Lord Jesus? Give verse from John 9 with your answer.

6. (Personal) Have you ever been tempted to "keep quiet" when God gives you an opportunity to speak out for Jesus Christ? Does the passage in Matthew 10:28-32 encourage you? Tell how it might encourage you to speak out for Christ.

FIFTH DAY: Read John 9:24-34.

1. What was the Pharisees' attitude and actions toward the man who could now see? What did they do? Give verses with your answer please.

2. How did the man respond to the Pharisees' insults to himself and to Jesus Christ? Give verses with your answer please. Try not to use John 9:31.

3. What according to John 9:31 did the healed man say?

4. **Challenge:** How do the following verses confirm what this man said in John 9:31?

   Psalm 34:15

   Psalm 66:18

   Proverbs 15:29

   Romans 12:2

5. (Personal) Which of the verses in question 4 was your favorite? Please write why it was your favorite verse.

6. According to John 9:34, what happened to the man born blind after he gave his truthful witness about Jesus Christ?

SIXTH DAY: Reread John 9:35-41.

1 a. Was Jesus Christ aware of what happened to this man?

  b. How did the Lord Jesus refer to Himself when He asked the man if he believed in Him?

  c. Did the Lord Jesus reveal Himself to this man? Give verse.

2. What was this man's response to the Lord Jesus?

3 a. (Personal) Have you ever revealed your faith to the Lord Jesus in this way?

  b. What does Romans 10:9 say that faith in Jesus Christ really involves?

4. What did the man do after he expressed his belief in the Lord Jesus? See John 9:38.

5. (Personal) If you believe in the Lord Jesus, how do you worship Him?

6. Which verse did you choose to memorize this week? Which verse meant the most to you personally? Write it down please.

THE GREAT I AM

John 9

Study Notes

Jesus Christ Is "I AM" John 8:51-59

Some of the Jewish leaders accused Jesus of having a demon because He claimed to be God (John 8:49). Jesus said, "Truly, truly, I say to you, if anyone keeps My word he shall never see death" (John 8:51).

The Jewish men asked, "Are you greater than our father Abraham, who died? . . . Who do you claim to be?" (John 8:53).

"Truly, truly, I say to you, before Abraham was, I AM" (John 8:58), Jesus replied.

As a result of this statement they took up stones to throw at Him but Jesus hid Himself and went out of the Temple. They were trying to stone the Lord Jesus Christ because He used the term, "I AM." This was the name that God used for Himself when He spoke to Moses (Exodus 3:1-14).

Have you ever stopped to think how useful your own name is? Imagine trying to get along without some designation that is peculiarly your own! Imagine trying to carry on a conversation with several people without being able to direct your remarks to the one specific person for whom they are meant. We have already discovered that John gives prominence to names and titles of our Lord Jesus Christ. Each one describes some quality of the nature of our Lord.

In this last section of John 8 the Lord Jesus is still in the treasury of the Temple at Jerusalem. Remember the Pharisees and the Scribes tried to trick Him with a question about the punishment of a woman who had been caught in the act of adultery. The Lord Jesus answered them in such a way that each one turned and went away.

Now the Lord speaks again to the Jewish people who attempt to argue with Him. In John 8:45 He says, "Because I tell the truth, you do not believe me." Also Jesus said, "He who is of God hears the words of God; the reason why you do not hear them is that you are not of God" (John 8:47). The Jews became so angry at these accusations that they lost their tempers. The idea that they, the children of Abraham, were children of the devil was unthinkable (John 8:44).

They in turn accused Jesus, "You [are] possessed by a demon" (John 8:48). What a terrible thing to say to the Son of God.

Calmly the Lord Jesus said, "Truly, truly, I say to you, if anyone keeps my word he shall never see death" (John 8:51). Never see death? This is impossible! All the prophets of the Old Testament were godly men, yet they died. Abraham was the head of the Jewish race, and he was dead. What kind of talk is this?

If a man keeps Jesus' saying, he shall never see death? Preposterous! No one but God is greater than Abraham. God gave Abraham the promises for the Jews. (Read Genesis 15:4-6, Genesis 17:1-8, Genesis 28:3-4). Does this Jesus think He is greater than Abraham? "Whom do you make yourself out to be?" the Jews asked (John 8:53).

Jesus replied, "If I honour myself, my honour is nothing: it is my Father that honoureth me; of whom ye say, that he is your God" (John 8:54). What a contrast the Lord presented. The Jews honored Abraham. But God gave honor to His Son, "It is My Father Who glorifies me—who extols Me, magnifies and praises Me." Jesus did not need honor from these people.

The Lord Jesus went a step further. Not only was He greater than Abraham, but He was also before Abraham. Most of the Jewish people did not honor Jesus Christ, but Abraham rejoiced to see His day (John 8:56).

The people said with contempt, "You are not yet fifty years old, and have You seen Abraham?" (John 8:57). How could Abraham rejoice to see the Lord Jesus' day when he had been dead for centuries?

Jesus replied using the name "I AM." "Truly, truly, I say to you, before Abraham was born, I AM" (John 8:58). The first time "I AM" was used by God is recorded in Exodus 3:1-14. One day while Moses was in the wilderness attending his father-in-law's sheep, he saw a bush on fire, yet the bush was not consumed. Moses went to the bush to see this strange sight.

God spoke out of the bush, introduced Himself, and told Moses that he was to bring the children of Israel out of Egypt, where they had been in slavery for over 400 years. Naturally, Moses was hesitant to accept so great a task. He asked the Lord, "Whom shall I say sent me?" (See Exodus 3:13.) On whose authority was he to go and speak to Pharaoh?

"And God said unto Moses, 'I AM THAT I AM . . . Thus shalt thou say unto the children of Israel, I AM hath sent me unto you" (Exodus 3:14). The name "I AM" was the name which God gave Himself. The Jewish people revered this name so much that they would not even pronounce it aloud when they read the Scriptures. One of the other names for God would be substituted.

So when the Jews heard the claim from the lips of Jesus, "Before Abraham was, I AM," they took up stones to kill Him. They fully understood that He had not only made Himself equal with God; He had declared Himself to be preexistent God. With those words, "I AM" He had told them that He was indeed "The Lord God, 'who is, and who was, and who is to come, the Almighty'" (Revelation 1:8.)

In other words, Jesus Christ had announced, "I am eternal. I am self-existent. I am God. In Me is life."

This declaration in John 8:58 is one of the greatest witnesses in all of John's Gospel to the deity of Christ. Yet sadly, God's chosen people, the Jews, did not believe Him. In fact, they were about to stone Him to death. But He went through their midst and disappeared.

What meaning does the name "I AM" have for us today? When Jesus Christ calls Himself "I AM," He is saying that He is the source of life. Our life is dependent upon others. We receive physical life from our parents. Our spiritual life is from our heavenly Father.

But Jesus Christ is different. He does not receive life; He gives life (John 14:6)! He does not look to God His Father to give Him life; in Him is life (John 1:4).

The Gospel of John was written to show that Jesus is God. By the use of a series of "I AMs" Christ proclaims His deity. He always used these I AM titles Himself. They were not given to Him by John or anyone else.

The I AMs

"*I am* the bread of life" (John 6:35). Can you imagine anyone but God making such a claim? It would sound foolish from anyone else. How can a person be bread? The Lord Jesus used the figure to show that you cannot live spiritually without Him any more than you can live physically without food. "I will satisfy your spiritual hunger," Jesus claimed. Those who come to Him learn that His claim is true.

"*I am* the light of the world" (John 8:12). We cannot live without light. We cannot walk without light. Jesus Christ claims, "I will show you the way to walk. If you follow me, you will never walk in darkness." He makes the same claim in John 9:5.

"Before Abraham was, *I am*" (John 8:58). Who but eternal God could ever make that claim? Christ is our God.

"*I am* the door" (John 10:7). Christ is the entrance to salvation. He is the only One who can save us from sin. He is the only door (John 3:16; Acts 4:12).

"*I am* the good shepherd" (John 10:11,14). Who of us does not need protection from evil and provision for our needs? Christ says, "I go before you. I lead the way. I am the entrance to the sheepfold. I look after my sheep. They have nothing to fear." (See Psalm 23.)

155

"*I am* the resurrection and the life" (John 11:25). Without Christ we could never face the future with confidence. We would be worried about what might happen some day. Jesus assures us that He will take us to be with Him. You have nothing to fear." Jesus says, "Because I live, ye shall live also" (John 14:19).

"*I am* the way, the truth, and the life" (John 14:6). Who can walk without a path? Who has any security without the truth? Who is content merely to exist without eternal life? Christ says, "I am the answer to all of these needs. Trust in me!"

"*I am* the true vine" (John 15:1). Who can live without the power and the strength Jesus Christ promised through the Holy Spirit who dwells within the Christian? The Lord knows our need and He promises us, "I am the vine, ye are the branches" (John 15:5).

Jesus Christ is saying to us through all of these, "I am your all. Apart from me, you can do nothing. Stay close by me moment by moment for life and for all you need to make your life abundant."

The Name of Jesus

Then there is the greatest of all names of our Lord. In Philippians 2:9-11 we read that God has "given him a name which is above every name: that at the name of Jesus every knee should bow, of things in heaven, and things in earth, and things under the earth; and that every tongue should confess that Jesus Christ is Lord, to the glory of God the Father." "For there is none other name under heaven given among men, whereby we must be saved" (Acts 4:12).

May each of us come to know the Lord Jesus better. May we let Him do for us the things He longs to do. He is the great I AM with all the power each of His titles indicates.

Jesus Heals the Man Born Blind John 9:1-12

We see the compassion of the Lord Jesus for a man who had been blind his entire life (John 9:1). As Jesus walked along the road, He saw someone who needed help. His disciples also saw the man but were concerned only with how he came to be blind (John 9:2). Jesus showed the power of God as He healed the man. The Lord Jesus was a busy person. Yet, He was never too busy to notice someone who needed Him and to minister to that person's need.

We often try to excuse our lack of concern for others with the comment, "I just don't have time." We ignore the work of missionaries because we are too concerned with our own wants. We overlook people living near us who may need our help because we are too busy with ourselves. Jesus was concerned, and He wants us to be concerned!

Each Christian should have a place of service in his church, in his civil government, in his neighborhood, among missionaries, in his business or wherever God calls him to service. How willing are you to respond when God nudges at your heart with someone's needs? "Are you a wise and faithful servant of the Lord? Have I given you the task of managing my household, to feed my children day by day? Blessings on you if I return and find you faithfully doing your work" (Matthew 24:45-46).

Do you hide your identity as a Christian? If so, you will not be able to awake others to the good news of Jesus Christ. Recently Prince Andrew, second son of Queen Elizabeth II and Prince Phillip, and an heir to the British throne, hid his identity from foreign students while studying French in Toulouse, France.

When asked who he was he told the class, "My name is Edward, my father is a gentleman farmer and my mother does not work."

Andrew and his 14 schoolmates spent three weeks at Caousou College. A Buckingham Palace spokesman said that only when the prince returned to England did they reveal his French connection. So his ruse worked!

Often Christians are afraid to identify themselves and play this same sort of game with people they meet along life's way. How much do your neighbors really know about you and your relationship to Jesus Christ? Are they aware of your faith through your consistent manner of life? Are they aware of your faith through a word spoken now and then, as the Holy Spirit gives you opportunity?

The Lord Jesus quickly stopped the disciples' question concerning the sin of this blind man (John 9:3). The Lord Jesus made it clear that we are not to judge people's sin; our task is to bring them to Jesus Christ. He also told His disciples that all sickness was not the result of a person's sin.

In John 9:5 Jesus again refers to Himself as "the light of the world." The Lord Jesus is drawing attention to the fact that He is about to give light to a man who has been born blind. John tells us of several healings which Jesus performed. The first of these, a nobleman's son, had probably been sick only a short time (John 4:46-54). The second is the man who had been lame for 38 years (John 5:1-16). This time the story concerns the healing of a man who had been blind from birth.

Jesus gave a definite command which the blind man had to obey. For him to do so was not easy. The Lord Jesus made clay of spit and soil and anointed the man's eyes with the clay. Then He told the man to wash in the Pool of Siloam (John 9:6,7).

The Pool of Siloam was in the southern part of the city. Imagine the blind man, with mud on his eyes, groping through the city, just to wash his face in this particular pool! It must have created quite a spectacle. But his faith and obedience were great enough to make him willing. He went to the pool as the Lord commanded. He washed and he saw (John 9:7).

The man groped his way to the pool, but he returned with the sure step of one who sees where he is going. It was such a change that some of the neighbors who had seen him before, looked with disbelief. "Is not this he that sat and begged?" (John 9:8).

"I am he," the fellow answered. He met Jesus Christ and was a changed person.

"What had happened?" (John 9:10). How is it that he could see?

"The man who is called Jesus made clay, and anointed my eyes, and said to me, 'Go to Siloam and wash'; so I went away and washed, and I received sight." This man did not know who Jesus was, just His name. This is the way the blind man described the One who had given him his sight (John 9:11).

The Pharisees Question the Man John 9:13-23

The Pharisees soon heard about the miracle, and the man was brought before them (John 9:13). It was the Sabbath day when Jesus made the clay and opened the man's eyes (John 9:14). The Lord Jesus performed another miracle on the Sabbath! He broke another of the Jewish traditions. Not only had He made clay, which was expressly forbidden on the Sabbath, but He had healed on the Sabbath also.

A person could give medical attention only if a life was in actual danger. And even then it must be such as to keep the patient from getting worse, and it must not make him any better! For instance, if a man had a toothache, he could not suck vinegar through his teeth because it could be considered sin. It was forbidden to set a broken limb—you couldn't even pour cold water over it or over a sprained hand or foot—for it would help heal!

Clearly, the man born blind was in no danger of losing his life; therefore, the Lord Jesus broke the man-made Sabbath laws when He healed him. It was by observation of these petty rules and details that the Scribes and Pharisees sought to honor God. To the Lord Jesus, the Pharisaical laws constituted an irreverent attitude toward men, whom God had created.

The Lord performed several miracles on the Sabbath day and each time He was met with strong opposition (Matthew 12:9-14; Mark 1:21-28; Mark 1:29-31; Luke 13:10-17; John 5:2-18; John 9:1-41). In each instance the Jewish authorities became angry when their tradition was broken. The fact that a person had been healed did not altar the situation. Their hearts were hardened to everything except their man-made law. As Christians, we need to enlarge our heart attitudes toward our fellowman's need.

When the Jews asked the man what he thought about the One who had healed him, he replied, "He is a prophet" (John 9:17). In order to shake his story, the religious leaders called the man's parents to confirm that he had indeed been blind. Fear of what might happen to them kept his parents quiet (John 9:19-23).

How many times does fear keep us from saying what we should about the Lord Jesus? We are afraid someone won't like us or that the particular group we are interested in may lose interest in us. When you should speak out for the Lord Jesus Christ, are you silent?

The Pharisees Question the Healed Man a Second Time John 9:24-34

When the parents would not speak, the Jewish leaders called the man back again. "Give God the praise:" they told him, "we know that this man is a sinner" (John 9:24). They could not doubt the miracle. After all, everyone knew that the man had been blind from birth, and it was plain to see that he now had sight. The leaders tried a new attack: "If you are really healed, then you should give the praise to God. Do not give it to this Man whom we know is a sinner."

The man answered, "Whether he is a sinner, I do not know; one thing I do know, that, whereas I was blind, now I see" (John 9:25). This time he had an answer that could not be questioned. He might not be able to answer all of their questions; he might not be able to argue as well as they. But here was an unanswerable statement. He had been blind all his life. Now, he stood before them seeing. There was no way to refute that fact!

Your personal testimony of what Jesus Christ has done for you is also unanswerable! You may lose the discussion argument; some clever person may succeed in backing you into a corner. But when you say, "This I know; I met Christ and He changed my life," you have stopped the argument!

The man's questioners may have been more educated than he, but his personal word still stood. However, they persisted, and in John 9:26 they asked him to repeat his story once again.

The man recognized that the leaders were floundering for a way to discount his testimony, for he entered into an argument with them. But this time it was he who backed them into a corner, "If this man were not of God, he could do nothing" (John 9:33). The man now realized that he was healed, not just by a man called Jesus, or even by a prophet, but he was healed by a man of God.

The Jews did all they could to make the blind man recant. When he would not, they kept their threat and cast him out of the synagogue (John 9:34).

159

Jesus Did Not Forget the Healed Man
John 9:35-41

The Lord Jesus did not forget the man. He gave the man sight and now He looked for him again. "When He had found him He said unto him, Dost thou believe on the Son of God?" (John 9:35). The man was now ready to believe in Jesus as his Lord, and he worshiped Him. First, he saw Jesus as a mere man, then later as a prophet; but now he recognized Jesus as the Son of God.

The Pharisees must have been following the man or the Lord Jesus, for now they gathered around while the Lord Jesus spoke to the man. His remark provoked a question from the Jews. They wanted to know if they were blind. They were blind to the fact that Jesus was the Messiah, the Son of God.

Jesus had come into the world that "they which see not might see" (John 9:39). This is not hard to understand for that is what happened to the blind man. But there's more to the statement than that. Far more important than opening the man's eyes is that Jesus opened his heart so that he recognized the Son of God and believed in Him. This man did not know who Jesus was when he first met Him, but before the episode ended, he worshiped Him as Lord (John 9:38).

The rest of the chapter is most unusual. The Lord Jesus came that those "which see might be made blind" (John 9:39). That is, all those, like the Pharisees, who claim spiritual sight but do not come to Christ, the light of the world, shall be shown to be blind spiritually. Only through Christ can anyone see the light, the will of God, and obey that will.

"Some Pharisees who were near, hearing this remark said to Him, Are we also blind?

"Jesus said to them, If you were blind, you would have no sin; but because you now claim to have sight, your sin remains.—If you were blind, you would not be guilty of sin; but because you insist, We do see [clearly], you are unable to escape your guilt" (John 9:40-41).

How does this lesson apply to you? Are you like that blind man? Not in physical blindness, but are you blind spiritually?

We are all sinners and we all need Jesus Christ to pass by our lives and give us light (Romans 3:23, Romans 6:23). The Lord Jesus may not work in everyone's life exactly the same way.

You may not come to Christ just like someone else. But the important thing is that God open your eyes of understanding and you go to the Lord to receive sight. When you do this, then you will see the joy, peace, happiness and abundant life God has prepared for you.

Study Questions

Before you begin your study this week:
1. Pray each day and ask God to speak to you through His Holy Spirit.
2. Use only your Bible to answer the following questions.
3. Write down your answers and, where called for, include the verses you used.
4. Challenge questions are for those who have the time and who wish to do them.
5. Personal questions are to be shared with the study group only if you wish to share.
6. As you study, look for a verse to memorize this week. Write it down, carry it with you, tack it to your bulletin board, tape it to the dashboard of your car. Make a real effort to learn the verse and its reference.

FIRST DAY: Read all of the preceding notes and look up all of the Scriptures given.

1. What was a helpful or new thought from the overview of John 8 and 9?

2. What personal application did you select to apply to your own life this week?

SECOND DAY: Read all of John 10 concentrating on John 10:1-14. Note: This is a parable told by Jesus to explain His relationship to, and care of, those who come to Him in faith, believing He is truly God's Son, their Savior and Lord.

1. What names does the Lord Jesus give Himself and what details does He tell about the names to explain this parable? Give verses please.

2 a. How does Isaiah 40:11 describe the Lord Jesus' tender care of His sheep (the Christians)? Put the verse into your own words if you wish to.

   b. (Personal) Think of the Lord as your own shepherd and reread Isaiah 40:11. How will you choose to ask Jesus Christ to tenderly care for you this week? Why not stop and pray about this now?

3. **Challenge:** Compare John 10:9-10 with John 14:6. How are they similar in their message?

4. **Challenge:** John 10:10 speaks of the abundant life which the Lord Jesus wants to give every Christian. How do the following verses help you to understand what He means by abundant life? Put the verses into your own words if you wish to, relating the promises to your life.

   2 Corinthians 6:4-8

   Philippians 4:4-7

Colossians 2:2-3

5. (Personal) Which of the above verses helped you to better understand the abundant life? Share with your discussion group, if possible, the reason why the verse helped you.

THIRD DAY: Read John 10:15-21.

1. Compare John 10:15 with Matthew 11:27. What similarities do you find?

2. What does the last part of John 10:15 and all of John 10:16 say?

3. **Challenge:** How does Revelation 5:8-9 help you to understand John 10:15-16? The Lamb in Revelation 5:8-9 is Jesus Christ. See also John 1:29 concerning the Lamb, the Lord Jesus Christ.

4 a. What interesting thing do you learn about prayer in the following verses?
   Revelation 5:8

   1 Chronicles 16:11

   b. (Personal) Do you need to make any changes in your prayer life? Does God have "golden vials" of the sweetness of your time spent in prayer with Him?

5. Write down everything Jesus Christ states about His death on the cross. "I lay down my life" is the wording Jesus Christ used for His death on the cross. Look in John 10:17-18 for your answer. Use your own words for the answer if you wish.

6. The Lord Jesus' words caused a division among the Jewish people who stood listening. What were the two viewpoints the Jewish people expressed? State them briefly. See John 10:19-21.

FOURTH DAY: Read John 10:22-30.

1 a. What time of the year was it and where was the Lord Jesus at this time?

b. What did the Jewish people ask the Lord Jesus?

c. What was the Lord Jesus' response to their question?

2. **Challenge:** Explain the name "my sheep" as the Lord Jesus uses it in John 10:26-27.

3. What do these verses say about the sheep and the shepherd? Put them into your own words, if you wish to.

Hebrews 13:20-21

1 Peter 2:24-25

4. What similarities do you find in comparing Hebrews 13:20-21 and 1 Peter 2:24-25 with Isaiah 53:5-6? If you have time, read all of Isaiah 53, for God led Isaiah to write about Jesus Christ suffering for us, in this chapter.

5. Looking back into John 10:28-29, what does the Lord Jesus say that He gives His sheep (those who trust in Him as Lord and Savior)?

6 a. (Personal) Have you ever received this great gift from Jesus Christ? Read Ephesians 1:7, Ephesians 2:8-9, and Revelation 3:20 to help you in your response to this question. Revelation 3:20 will help you know how to respond to the Lord Jesus Christ.

b. If you have received the Lord Jesus by faith, how are you sharing Him with others? Are you sharing this good news in some way? Will you pray and ask God to show you new and exciting opportunities to share the Lord Jesus in your business, home, church, neighborhood and city?

FIFTH DAY: Read John 10:31-42.

1. What did the Jews intend to do to the Lord Jesus after He had declared that God was His Father and said that they were "one"? See John 10:29-31.

2. What question did the Lord Jesus ask these men as they stood with the stones in their hands?

3. What was the real reason the Jewish people had decided to stone Jesus? Did His question in John 10:32 provoke an honest answer from the crowd?

4. What similar thing happened in John 5:16-18?

5 a. What very important thing does the Lord Jesus say about Scripture in John 10:35?

b. What does the Lord Jesus say in John 10:38 which shows His complete "oneness" and equality with the Father?

c. What does the Lord Jesus pray in John 17:20-23 which again reminds us of His "oneness" with the Father?

d. (Personal) Do you find some personal challenge for your life this week in John 17:20-23? If so, please write it down and share with your discussion group, if possible.

6. The Lord Jesus escaped from the stoning. Where did He go and what encouraging words do you find in the last sentence of John 10?

SIXTH DAY: Read Psalm 23 with John 10:10 in mind.

Put down your favorite verses and give the key thought which blessed you in the verse. You may use your own words if you wish. Everyone will have different verses and reasons for using them, so perhaps you could volunteer to share your favorite verse from the Psalm. Tell why you chose it. You will not be called upon if you do not wish to share.

THE GOOD SHEPHERD

John 10

Study Notes

The Parable of the Good Shepherd
John 10:1-14

The ministry of Jesus Christ was coming to a close. Just as a snowball rolling down a hill gets bigger and bigger and goes faster and faster, so was the work of Jesus in Jerusalem. Opposition to Jesus Christ was getting stronger. More hatred for the Lord Jesus was being voiced. With the opposition came the testimony of those who did believe in Jesus Christ. Often this is the case! When the road gets hard, we gain the strength to stand firm (2 Corinthians 12:10; 2 Thessalonians 1:4).

John 10 continues the narrative of chapter 9. The Lord Jesus had just *told* the Pharisees that they were not able to lead the people because they did not come to Him, the light of the world (John 9:41). Now, Jesus proceeds to *show* them how blind they really are.

He tells them a story about Himself. He tells them about those who believe in Him, and of the Pharisees who are false leaders of the people (John 10:6). Jesus Christ proved His point. The Pharisees were so blind that they could not understand the message He gave.

If we are to fully understand the Lord Jesus' reference to Himself as a Shepherd, we really need to know that God, in the Old Testament, is often pictured as a Shepherd and the people as His flock. "We thy people and sheep of thy pasture will give thee thanks for ever" (Psalm 79:13). There are many other references to God being the Shepherd, and the people as His flock: Psalm 23:1, Psalm 77:20, Psalm 80:1, Psalm 95:7, Psalm 100:3, Isaiah 40:11.

This thought is carried over into the New Testament as Jesus depicts Himself as the Good Shepherd (John 10:11). He is the Shepherd who will risk His life to seek and to save the one straying sheep (Matthew 18:12, Luke 15:4). The Lord Jesus calls His disciples the little flock (Luke 12:32). We read in Mark 14:27 and Matthew 26:31 that when He, the Shepherd, is smitten (His death upon the cross), the sheep "shall be scattered." In 1 Peter 2:25 He is referred to as the Shepherd of the Souls of Men, and in Hebrews 13:20 as the Great Shepherd of the Sheep.

Let's look at the parable and see if we can do better than the Pharisees did in understanding Jesus' teaching. In John 10:1,2, Jesus speaks about a door to a sheepfold, thieves and robbers, the shepherd and the sheep. The illustration He uses is that of an oriental sheepfold, a portion of land surrounded by a fence or wall.

The Caring Shepherd

In Palestine the sheep are primarily kept for their fleece to make woolen cloth. Therefore, they may be with the shepherd for years. They often have names by which the shepherd calls them; usually their names are descriptive—"Brown-legs," "Black-spotted." The shepherd goes ahead of the sheep to see that the path is safe and that there are no dangers.

It is only through the Lord Jesus that men can find access to God.

Sometimes the sheep have to be encouraged to follow. The sheep understand their own shepherd's voice because he uses a special kind of sing-song language to speak to them. It is an uncanny noise of animal sounds arranged in a kind of order and has nothing human about it. No sooner does the shepherd make these sounds than an answering bleat shivers across the herd.

The Lord Jesus spoke of thieves and robbers (John 10:1). In the villages and towns there were communal sheepfolds where all the village flocks were sheltered when they returned home at night. Here they were protected by a strong door; only the guardian of the door held the key. It is this kind of fold that Jesus refers to in John 10:3, "The gatekeeper opens the gate for him, and the sheep hear his voice and come to him; and he calls his own sheep by name and leads them out."

When the sheep were out on the hills during the warm season, they did not return to the village at night. Instead they were collected into sheepfolds which were just open spaces enclosed by rock walls.

An open space in the walled enclosure let the sheep go in and out, but there was no door of any kind. At night the shepherd himself lay across the opening so that none of the sheep could get out and no other animal could get into the fold except over his body.

Therefore, in this sheepfold the shepherd was indeed the door. There was no access to the sheepfold except through him! That was what the Lord Jesus was referring to when He said, "I am the door" (John 10:7). It is only through the Lord Jesus that men can find access to God. "Through him," said Paul, "we both have access by one Spirit unto the Father" (Ephesians 2:18). "[He is the] new and living way" (Hebrews 10:20). The Lord Jesus opens the way to God.

Jesus Christ is the only door. He is not just one of many ways to God. He is the only way. You do not have a choice.

Some people will say that every man has a right to choose his own way to God; that there are many ways and each person chooses the way that fits him best. This idea that "all roads lead to God" is not true. Jesus Christ said, "I am the door" (John 10:7). He did not say, "I am *a* door," but "I am *the* door."

When the Lord Jesus spoke of thieves and robbers, He spoke of those of His day who were false teachers. They were the Pharisees who had confused the people and taught them lessons that were not true. False teachers in our day also confuse people with lessons which are not true.

The Lord Jesus Christ has preserved the Bible, His Word, to teach us. In it is "the truth" (John 14:6). "All scripture is inspired by God and profitable for teaching, for reproof, for correction, for training in righteousness; that the man of God may be adequate, equipped for every good work" (2 Timothy 3:16). For this reason it is important that we know the Word of God.

A good shepherd protects his sheep even though it may jeopardize his own life. When David wrote Psalm 23, he knew that the Good Shepherd would never leave him. "Thou art with me," David wrote. That is what Jesus said, "I am the good shepherd: the good shepherd giveth his life for the sheep" (John 10:11). If you are one of His sheep, He will never leave you.

The Faithful Shepherd

Shepherds are so faithful that when savage beasts or thieves come, the faithful shepherd often puts his life in jeopardy to defend his flock. In more than one case the shepherd has had to literally lay down his life in the contest. One shepherd, instead of fleeing, fought with three Bedouin robbers until he was hacked to pieces with their khanjars. He died among the sheep he was defending.

A true shepherd would never hesitate to risk his life for the sheep, even to death. The sheep become his friends and companions. It is second nature for him to think of them before he thinks of himself.

A false shepherd comes into the job, not as a calling, but as a means of making money. The Lord Jesus, speaking of the false shepherd, says that when the wolf comes, "He . . . leaves the sheep, and flees, and the wolf snatches them, and scatters them. He flees because he is a hireling, and is not concerned about the sheep" (John 10:12,13).

The Lord Jesus Christ is telling us that in this world there will be false shepherds and we need to be on guard against them. The best way to recognize a false shepherd is to know the Good Shepherd, the Lord Jesus Christ, and to know His Word, the Bible.

Because we are weak, helpless sheep, not wise enough to find our own way, we need to trust our lives to the guidance of the Good Shepherd. "And when he putteth forth his own sheep, he goeth before them, and the sheep follow him" (John 10:4). He searches out the safe paths for us and He goes ahead! As someone has so beautifully said, "Christ is in all the tomorrows that we will have to journey through. We may be sure, therefore, that all is safe farther ahead where He is leading."

When we have committed our way to the Lord and are trusting fully in Him, we don't need to worry about being on the wrong road.

Recently I saw a cartoon of a couple in a car winding along a back road. The man, who was driving, said to his wife, "I think we're on the wrong road, but we're making such good time, let's just keep right on going!"

God will keep us and guide us faithfully and unerringly and give us an abundant life when we are fully committed to Him (John 10:10). Though we know we're to commit everything to the Lord, we often forget to leave our burdens with the Lord!

Don't Worry

Experts estimate that of the things that worry the average individual, 40 percent of them will probably never happen; 30 percent of them have already happened. (All the worry in the world can't change what has happened!) That takes care of 70 percent of the worry! Twelve percent are needless worries about health; 10 percent are considered petty and trivial. Last of all, possibly no more than eight percent of all the things that worry us deserve our concern. The trick is to determine what part of the 100 percent is really deserving of our worry and concentrate on resolving that part with God's help.

"For I know in whom I have believed, and am persuaded that he is able to keep that which I have committed unto him against that day" (2 Timothy 1:12). This is the peace we can have in the abundant life that God has promised us in John 10:10. In Psalm 55:22 God urges us to "cast thy burden upon the Lord." In other words, we are really to

One of the kindest things that God does for us is to limit the distance we can see into our tomorrows!

unload it fully on Him, and He will take care of it. Contentment in life, the abundant life, can come in no other way.

Strength for Each Day

One of the kindest things that God does for us is to limit the distance we can see into our tomorrows! As an example, it is a fact that it is easier to ride a bicycle uphill at night than during the day. The reason is that at night the bicycle headlight permits the rider to see only a few feet at a time ahead of him. So he keeps pedaling forward in the path of the light. In the daytime, he can see the hill, and it may seem totally insurmountable.

Similarly, a great task which faces us may appear impossible to tackle. But when we break it down into smaller portions we find that the task is conquerable! So it is as we commit ourselves to the Lord. He will give us the strength to achieve His great plan for our lives each day.

The Abundant Life

The Lord Jesus Christ, our Good Shepherd, gave His life that He might give us an abundant life (John 10:10,11). He died for His sheep. His death was sacrificial. He did not die on His own behalf; He died for you and me. (Read John 3:16,17; Romans 3:24-26; Romans 4:25; Romans 5:1,6,8-11, Galatians 1:4.)

All through the Old Testament, as animals were sacrificed to God and forgiveness was asked for sin, their death was a picture of what Jesus Christ would do for the sin of the world. He died for everyone. But only those who accept His sacrifice and receive Him as their Savior will have their sins forgiven and receive eternal, abundant life (John 10:1).

Are you willing to open your life to God so that He can take each

171

day's circumstances and make them a blessing in your life and in the lives of others? "Jesus Christ the same yesterday, and today, and for ever" (Hebrews 13:8). He is waiting to help you. Open your life to the Good Shepherd, and let Him provide you with the abundant life (John 10:10) in the midst of your circumstances.

The Explanation of the Parable Causes Division John 10:15-21

The Lord Jesus Christ explains to the crowd gathered round Him that, since the Father knows His Son and the Son knows the will of His Father, the Father knows that He can count on His Son's obedience to lay down His life for the sheep. Hebrews 13:20,21 speaks of the Lord Jesus, the Great Shepherd of the sheep, who not only lays down His life for His sheep but also equips us to do the will of God. The Lord Jesus spoke of the abundant life in John 10:10. The only way to know an abundant life is to do the will of God and obey His plan for our lives.

"And now may the God of peace, who brought again from the dead our Lord Jesus, equip you with all you need for doing his will. May he who became the great Shepherd of the sheep by an everlasting agreement between God and you, signed with his blood, produce in you through the power of Christ all that is pleasing to him. To him be glory forever and ever. Amen" (Hebrews 13:20,21). Also see Romans 8:32.

In John 10:16 we discover that there are other sheep for whom the Lord Jesus Christ came. "I must bring them also, and they will heed my voice; and there will be one flock with one shepherd." By this statement the Lord Jesus makes it plain that in addition to coming to the Jewish people, His own nation, He was also to go out into all the world to call people from all nations to put their trust in Him. People other than Jews, are known as Gentiles.

Many ask why the Lord Jesus came first to His own, the Jewish people. The ultimate aim of the Lord Jesus is to win the world for God, but as any great commander knows, he must first start with a limited objective. If He had tried to attack on too wide a front, He would only have scattered His forces. So, in order to win a complete victory, He began by concentrating His forces in a limited area, the Jewish race. When He sent out His disciples, He deliberately chose a limited objective and at first sent them only to the Jewish people (Matthew 10:5).

The Lord Jesus was deliberately concentrating on the Jewish nation, but His ultimate aim was the gathering of the whole world to God through faith in Jesus Christ. In His last message to the 11 disciples when they went to Galilee, into the mountains, Jesus Christ said,

"All authority in heaven and on earth has been given to me. Go there-fore and make disciples of all nations, baptizing them in the name of the Father and of the Son and of the Holy Spirit, teaching them to observe all that I have commanded you; and lo, I am with you always, to the close of the age" (Matthew 28:18-20). It is only in Jesus Christ that all nations, all races, all classes of people can become one. It is only through His person that barriers can be removed as people are unified by faith in the Lord Jesus Christ.

Let's look back at John 10:17 where Jesus says, "I lay down my life, that I might take it again." The Good Shepherd died for us, but He is not dead now. He died, but He arose again on the third day. He is a living Savior! (Read Romans 6:4-10; Acts 1:3,22; Acts 10:40,41.) "But if the spirit of him that raised up Jesus from the dead dwell in you, he that raised up Christ from the dead shall also quicken your mortal bodies by his Spirit that dwelleth in you" (Romans 8:11).

Yes, the good shepherd protects his sheep! He protects even though it means his life. David knew this when he wrote Psalm 23. David knew that the Good Shepherd would never leave him alone. "Thou art with me," David wrote. That is also true for us. "For he hath said, I will never leave thee, nor forsake thee. So that we may boldly say, The Lord is my helper, and I will not fear what man will do unto me" (Hebrews 13:5,6).

All of these remarks by the Lord Jesus caused a division among the Jews. Many of them felt He had a demon and was completely mad. Others said, "These are not the sayings of a man possessed by a demon. Can a demon open the eyes of the blind?" (John 10:21).

This is the third time in the Gospel of John that we read that there was a division created by the Lord Jesus among His hearers (John 7:43, 9:16). Most felt that the Lord was demonized and unworthy of listening to, while a few were impressed by the words He spoke, and with the recollection of the miracle performed on the blind man (John 9:1-12).

The Deity of Christ John 10:22-42

The Lord Jesus was walking on Solomon's porch (John 10:23). An interval of about two months separated this occasion from the events in the preceding verses in John 10. The Feast of Tabernacles was commemorated in the fall, and the Feast of the Dedication in winter (John 7:2, John 10:22). The Feast of the Dedication memorialized the cleansing and rededication of the temple by Judas Maccabaeus after the sacrilege committed by Antiochus Epiphanes, in the year 165 B.C.

The Lord Jesus was accosted by some of the Jewish people as He walked in Solomon's Porch, located in the eastern portion of the

Court of the Gentiles, the largest court in the Temple area. It surrounded the inner court and the very Temple itself.

These Jewish people came to Him again saying, Are you really the Christ? Jesus said that He had already told them that He was, but they didn't believe Him (John 10:25). He repeated that if these Jews were His sheep they would hear His voice and follow Him (John 10:26-27). But they did not know God.

Do you hear His voice? Does He know you? Do you follow Him? If you are His sheep and He is your Shepherd you do all of these things.

Jesus goes on to say, "And I give unto them eternal life; and they shall never perish, neither shall any man pluck them out of my hand" (John 10:28). That sounds like John 3:16. The Lord Jesus holds His sheep in His hand (John 10:29). How wonderful to know that we are loved by God and to know He holds on to us!

Let God Hold On to You

One day a little girl went walking with her father. "Let me take your hand; the streets are covered with ice and snow," the father said.

But the little girl shook her head. She could do it all right by herself. Just then her feet slid out from under her and down she went. She got up and then turned to her father.

"Let me hold your hand," she said.

That was a little better. But when they came to a slippery place she let go and down she went again! That was all she needed.

"You can take my hand," she said.

Her father took it and held it tightly in his. The next time the little girl slipped, her father held her tight. Her legs churned in the air for a few seconds, but soon, with her father's help, she got them where they belonged, and the two of them walked on.

Learn the spiritual implication of this illustration. You can't walk alone; you'll stumble and fall. You can't hold on to God; you'll get tired and let go. Let God hold on to you, as He has proposed, He will never get tired, "For the Lord will be your confidence, and will keep your foot from being caught" (Proverbs 3:26).

"Hear, my son, and accept my words, that the years of your life may be many. I have taught you the way of wisdom; I have led you in the paths of uprightness. When you walk, your step will not be hampered; and if you run, you will not stumble. Keep hold of instruction, do not let go; guard her, for she is your life" (Proverbs 4:10-13).

Follow the Shepherd

In John 10:30 Jesus again claims that He and His Father are the same.

He is equal with God. Sadly, the effect of His words on the people was anger, for they responded in unbelief (John 10:31) and again attempted to stone the Lord Jesus. But He escaped and they were unsuccessful in their attempt to kill Him. (John 10:39). Remember no one could take Jesus' life from Him (John 10:18).

The Lord went into the province of Perea, near to Bethabara, where John had first been baptized. See if you can find this area on the map at the back of your Bible, or on some other Holy Land map. The whole controversy over the authority of the Lord Jesus Christ ended with a note of victory! "And many believed in him there" (John 10:42).

As we think back over this chapter in John, how do you fit into the picture? Is Jesus Christ your Shepherd? You'll have to be one of His sheep if you want Him to be your Shepherd. If He is your Shepherd, do you listen for His voice?

Do not follow the thieves and robbers! Do not pay any attention to them. Follow wherever your Shepherd leads. He walks before you. He never takes you any place where He has not gone. Let Him be your guide. Use the Bible to help you learn the way He wants you to walk.

This study provides a daily plan for you to spend time with God in prayer and in His Word, the Bible. Will you choose to spend a small portion of each day with your Shepherd? He wants to save and protect you, lead you and bless you. What will you do? It is up to you!

Study Questions

Before you begin your study this week:

1. Pray each day and ask God to speak to you through His Holy Spirit.
2. Use only your Bible to answer the following questions.
3. Write down your answers and, where called for, include the verses you used.
4. Challenge questions are for those who have the time and who wish to do them.
5. Personal questions are to be shared with your study group only if you wish to share.
6. As you study, look for a verse to memorize this week. Write it down, carry it with you, tack it to your bulletin board, tape it to the dashboard of your car. Make a real effort to learn the verse and its reference.

FIRST DAY: Read all of the preceding notes and look up all of the Scriptures given.

1. What was a helpful or new thought from the overview of John 10?

2. What personal application did you select to apply to your own life this week?

SECOND DAY: Read all of John 11 concentrating on John 11:1-16.

1 a. Who was sick? How was he related to Mary and Martha? What place was he from?

b. How is Mary identified in John 11:2 and John 12:3?

c. How is Mary identified in John 11:2 and John 12:3?

2 a. What did the Lord Jesus say when He received the message from Mary and Martha saying that Lazarus, whom He loved, was sick? Give the verse.

b. How long did the Lord Jesus stay in the same place after He received the message that Lazarus was sick?

c. **Challenge:** Why do you think He waited so long before starting out to help His sick friend? Read John 11:4; John 11:11 and John 11:40-45 to help you think about your answer.

3. (Personal) Has the Lord Jesus ever said, "Wait," before answering a prayer of yours? Could you relate this experience to John 11:4 and John 11:40? Share if possible an experience you had of sending a message of prayer to the Lord Jesus and how His delay eventually brought glory to God and to Himself.

4 a. The disciples were worried about the Lord Jesus' safety in Judea (where Bethany was located). See John 7:3,10,44 and John 8:59, and John 10:39,40 if you do not remember the attacks and stonings that some of the Jewish people attempted the last time the Lord Jesus was in Judea. What was the Lord Jesus' reply to the disciples' expressions of concern for His safety? See John 11:9.

b. **Challenge:** The Christian's day can be considered as 12 hours of light each day. How do the following verses help you to know how to walk as a Christian? Put them into your own words.

Psalm 119:130

Proverbs 6:23

1 John 1:7

5. (Personal) Which of the verses in question 4b meant the most to you in your Christian walk today or helped you the most? Share your favorite verse and tell why it blessed your heart.

6 a. How did Thomas, called "doubter" (John 14:5,6; John 20:25,27), show great courage by being willing to go to Judea and die with Christ at this time? Give verse in John 11.

b. **Challenge:** What does Colossians 3:2,3 give you as encouragement as a Christian for the value of your own life?

THIRD DAY: Read John 11:17-27.

1. How long had Lazarus been in the grave by the time Jesus Christ arrived at Bethany?

2. **Challenge:** Though the Christian's body is placed in the grave, the "real person" goes to be with God because of his faith in Jesus Christ, God's Son. The following verses speak of this. You may put them in your own words if you wish, and insert your name into the verse to assert your faith in Jesus Christ and the truth of these statements in the Scriptures.

Psalm 73:23,24

3. (Personal) Which verse in question 2 brought you the most joy and hope about your eternal life with God? Tell why. Share with your discussion group if possible.

4. How did Martha reveal her deep faith in Jesus Christ in John 11:21,22?

5. **Challenge:** What resurrection was Martha thinking of when she replied to Jesus Christ in John 11:23,24? See Daniel 12:2.

6. The Lord Jesus was not speaking of the resurrection of the body but of the spirit. Put your name in John 11:25,26 as you write these verses. Is this your statement of faith?

FOURTH DAY: Read John 11:28-37.

1 a. How did Martha declare her faith in the Lord Jesus Christ in John 11:27?

   b. (Personal) If you believe as Martha did, how could you share this truth with others? Please share your thoughts with your discussion group, if possible.

2 a. When Mary heard that her Master (the Lord Jesus) had called her, how did she obediently respond? Give verse.

b. How does Joshua 1:8 suggest that we can be successful in obeying God, and what blessings are promised to those who obey Him? Put this into your own words.

3. **Challenge:** We need God's power if we are to be obedient to His Word and to His plan for us. What do the following verses say concerning the Holy Spirit's power in the Christian's life?

Zechariah 4:6

Acts 9:31

4. (Personal) Which of these verses concerning the Holy Spirit would you like to claim for your life this week? Write down why you chose the verse. Please share with your group, if possible.

5. Look at John 11 again. Where did the Jewish mourners, who were with Mary in the house, think she had gone when she ran out to meet the Lord Jesus?

6 a. What did the Lord Jesus do in John 11:35?

b. Do you think it is wrong to teach boys that they should show very little emotion? Is it physically, emotionally or spiritually good or bad for yourself and for others to hold in all emotion?

FIFTH DAY: Read John 11:38-44.

1. What was Martha's response to the Lord Jesus when He asked that the stone be rolled back from Lazarus' grave?

2. Of what did the Lord Jesus remind Martha in John 11:40?

3 a. **Challenge:** The Lord Jesus Christ was challenging Martha to trust in Him and His Word. What do the following verses say about trusting God? Put them into your own words and insert your name in the promise.

Psalm 37:5

Psalm 118:8

Proverbs 3:5

   b. (Personal) Which of these verses on trust would you like to claim for your life this week? Write the reason why you choose to claim this promise from God's Word. Share with your discussion group.

4. The Lord Jesus prayed in John 11:41,42. What did He thank God for and why did He say He gave God the thanks?

5. There are many Scriptures in both the Old and New Testament which tell us that God hears and answers prayer. What do Psalm 34:15,17 say to encourage you to pray more often and about everything?

6. How did the Lord call Lazarus from his tomb in John 11:43?

SIXTH DAY: Read John 11:44-57.

1 a. How did Lazarus come out of the tomb?

   b. What did the Lord Jesus tell the crowd around the tomb to do for Lazarus?

   c. What was the result of this miracle? See John 11:45.

   d. What was another result of this miracle? See John 11:46.

2. What did the Pharisees fear? See John 11:48.

3. Caiaphas, the high priest, did not realize that God used him to speak prophetic words about the sacrificial death of Jesus Christ for all nations, peoples, and races. What did he say in John 11:50?

4. **Challenge:** How does 1 Thessalonians 5:9,10 fulfill what Caiaphas said in John 11:50?

5 a. What did the Pharisees plan to do about Jesus Christ after Caiaphas made his statement in John 11:51,52?

   b. What did the Lord Jesus do as a result of the Pharisees' plan? Give the verse.

   c. See if you can find Ephraim on your Bible map. Also locate Bethany where Mary, Martha and Lazarus lived.

6. Which verse helped you the most this week? Did you underline this verse in your Bible? Are you going to hide this promise of God in your heart by memorizing it?

THE RESURRECTION AND THE LIFE

John 11

Study Notes

Lazarus Dies; the Lord Goes to His Home John 11:1-6

Have you ever wished that you could turn back the clock? Perhaps you had such a good time last summer that you would like to live your vacation over again! Or maybe you made a wrong choice about something and you would like a chance to correct your mistake.

The Lord Jesus Christ never wanted to turn back the clock when He was on earth. There was no need to! The Lord Jesus always knew exactly what He was doing and He always acted at just the right time. But, to everyone concerned with the events in John 11, it seemed that the Lord's timing was wrong. But He knew He was right!

The Lord Jesus was moving closer and closer to the time of His death. The events of John 11 probably took place within three months of the Crucifixion during the last winter of Jesus' life. In John 10:40 we read that the Lord Jesus had gone into the province of Perea (in present-day Jordan). Find this area on your Bible map. While Jesus was in Perea, a messenger came to Him and brought Him the news of the illness of His friend, Lazarus (John 11:3). When the Lord Jesus received this message His thoughts must have gone directly to this family and to their home where He had often received rest, understanding, peace and love. He had no home of His own, nowhere to lay His head (Luke 9:58). Yet, when He was near Bethany, the Lord

Jesus had just such a place where He could occasionally go and find people who loved Him (Luke 10:38-42).

As Christians we need to keep in mind that one of the greatest gifts we can give one another is the gift of understanding and peace. To have someplace to go to get away from the tensions of life, where the atmosphere is relaxed and peaceful, is a lovely thing. We need to open our own homes and apartments like Mary, Martha and Lazarus did. It need not cost a lot of money nor demand lavish hospitality. It requires only a warm and understanding heart!

Lazarus, the brother of Mary and Martha, was sick. The sisters sent word to the Lord Jesus that Lazarus was ill (John 11:3) but their message included no request that Jesus come to Bethany. They knew that such a request was unnecessary for they realized the simple statement that they were in need would bring the Lord Jesus to them. They knew that He had a solution to the anxiety that gripped them, for their friendship with the Lord Jesus had given them confidence of His goodness and power.

Mary and Martha immediately sent their message to the Lord Jesus Christ. When we are in need do we immediately take all our needs to the Lord Jesus Christ through prayer?

Faith in Prayer

Andrew Murray suggests two ways that we look at prayer: from the human viewpoint and from the divine viewpoint. It makes a vast difference which view rules your prayer life. In the human viewpoint, we come to God thinking about our own needs and desires, our efforts to pray, the time we spend in prayer. Our faith in the results is expressed as we experience answers to our askings.

In the divine viewpoint we regard prayer in the light of the God of love who is all-powerful. We come to Him who encourages us to bring Him our needs and desires. We approach Him as the one who has an interest in every phase of our life. He has designed all things for our greatest good (Romans 8:28,29).

His faithfulness never wavers. (Read Deuteronomy 7:9, Psalm 89:1, 1 Peter 4:19.) God's greatest desire is our growth in Christ's likeness. He honors our faith and waits to answer our prayers.

Facing a Crisis

Jesus loved Mary, Martha and Lazarus. He loved them, yet He did not hurry to see them. He wanted them to see a greater display of His glory and power than they ever dreamed of. He waited two days after He received the message of Lazarus' illness.

When Jesus arrived in Bethany, Lazarus had been dead for four days. The Lord Jesus waited until there was no possibility that Lazarus would be alive when He arrived. (John 11:4). When Jesus called forth Lazarus from the dead it was for "the glory of God, that the Son of God might be glorified thereby."

The death of Lazarus became the cause of his sister's grief, but his emergence from the grave gave them reason to rejoice and led to many receiving the Lord Jesus Christ by faith. So it is now! The presence and power of Christ can so alter circumstances that they become the means of blessing to many.

We must choose to walk in the light of Jesus Christ rather than in the darkness of self-will and separation from Him.

In John 11:7-16 the Lord Jesus told His disciples that He was going to return to Judea; the disciples were afraid He was going to His death (John 11:8). His life had been threatened in Judea (John 8:59, John 10:39) and His life would be in real danger now! The Lord assured the disciples that, in going to Judea He knew exactly what He was doing.

The Lord Jesus said, "Are there not twelve hours in the day? If any man walk in the day, he stumbleth not, because he seeth the light of this world." The Lord Jesus Christ's reply to His disciples in John 11:9 applied both to Himself and to His followers. He could safely go back to Judea as long as He was walking in the light of His Father's will. His enemies could not touch Him until His hour had come (Matthew 26:44-50).

Then for a short time the darkness of spiritual opposition would be permitted to close in on Jesus Christ. The lesson for the disciples, as well as for us, is that we must choose to walk in the light of Jesus Christ rather than in the darkness of self-will and separation from Him. We will stumble (John 11:10) when we walk without the light of Jesus Christ. Read James 4:14-17, Proverbs 6:23.

The disciples did not really understand that Lazarus was dead. They thought that he was asleep. The Lord Jesus had to say definitely, "Lazarus is dead" (John 11:14) before they realized the truth. He went on to say, "I am glad for your sakes that I was not there, to the intent ye may believe; nevertheless let us go unto him" (John 11:15). He was telling His disciples that He was glad that this experience of sorrow would eventually bring them to full faith in His Lordship. A saying that is appropriate here can also be applied to our own lives. "God often digs wells of joy with the spade of sorrow!"

Notice the courage with which Thomas responded (John 11:16). Thomas seemed to think that to go to Judea would mean Jesus' death, but he was willing and ready to die with his Lord. This can be applied to our own Christian lives in a spiritual way. "Let heaven fill your thoughts; don't spend your time worrying about things down here. You should have as little desire for this world as a dead person does. Your real life is in heaven with Christ and God. And when Christ who is our real life comes back again, you will shine with him and share in all his glories" (Colossians 3:2-4).

The real life that we have is hid with Christ in God. Thomas must have sensed his life being hidden with Christ in God and this is what gave him the courage to obediently go with our Lord Jesus to Judea and if need be to die with Him there. This was a crisis, and Thomas was willing to face it in the strength of his Lord (see Philippians 4:13).

Sir John Reith once said, "I do not like crises; but I like the opportunities which they supply." The death of Lazarus, a crisis, brought an opportunity for Jesus to demonstrate the power of God in a most amazing way (John 11:4). Thomas also faced a crisis and welcomed it as an opportunity to trust Christ further. For each of us a crisis should be an opportunity! Do you think of your crises in this way?

The Lord Jesus Speaks to Martha and Mary John 11:17-37

In order to visualize the scene, let us describe a Jewish house of mourning. Normally in Palestine burial followed death as quickly as possible. This was necessary because of the warm climate, and no embalming as we know it at this time. However, the finest spices and ointments were used to anoint the body; the body itself was clothed in the most magnificent robes. Valuable treasures and possessions were also put in the tomb. The funeral and burial were exceedingly costly.

About the middle of the first century people began to rebel against this custom because it had become an intolerable burden. The man who changed the burial customs was the famous rabbi called Gamaliel II. He gave orders that he was to be buried in a simple linen robe, and thus broke the extravagant funeral tradition. Thereafter, it became the custom to wrap the body in a simple linen dress which was sometimes called by the beautiful name, "the traveling-dress."

Many people attended the funeral in courtesy and respect for the deceased and his family. Women mourners went ahead of the procession to the tomb where memorial speeches were made. Everyone was expected to express the deepest sympathy. The family left the tomb first and passed between two long lines of mourners. A wise rule was followed—the mourners were not to be tormented by useless and idle talk. One custom, very similar to today, was that a meal was prepared and served by the friends of the family on the return from the tomb. This meal consisted of bread, hard-boiled eggs and lentils. The round eggs and lentils symbolized life which was always rolling toward death.

As soon as the body was carried out of the house, all of the furniture was moved and the mourners sat on the ground or on low stools. A period of deep mourning lasted seven days; the first three were days of weeping. During the entire seven days the mourners were forbidden to wash, to put on shoes, or to engage in any study or business. After the week of deep mourning, was a 30-day period of lighter mourning. When Jesus found a crowd in the house at Bethany, He found what would be expected in a Jewish house of mourning.

Show Concern and Care

A sacred duty of the Jewish people was to express loving sympathy with the sorrowing friends and relatives of one who had died. Visits of sympathy to the sick and to the sorrowing were an essential part of the Jewish religion. Deuteronomy 13:4 says, "Ye shall walk after the Lord your God." In the Scriptures we find examples of God's loving care and concern for His people.
1. God clothed the naked (Genesis 3:21).
2. God visited the sick (Genesis 18:1).
3. God comforted the mourners (Genesis 25:11).
4. God buried the dead (Deuteronomy 34:6).
This is a pattern we can all follow as we trust the Holy Spirit to minister through us to others. Let us make note that it is our Christian duty to show sympathy, concern and care for a mourner.

Jesus Consoles Martha

Martha heard that Jesus was coming and ran out to meet Him. Here Martha shows her true character. When Luke tells about Martha and Mary (Luke 10:38-42) he shows Martha as one who loved action. Martha said to Jesus in John 11:21, "Lord, if you had been here, my brother would not have died."

The way Martha said those words made them sound as if she were scolding the Lord for His delay. But then, she quickly added "Even now, whatsoever thou wilt ask of God, God will give it thee" (John 11:22).

The Lord Jesus Christ reassured Martha by saying, "Thy brother shall rise again." The Lord may have been referring to what He was about to do. But if He was, Martha did not understand. She looked toward some far distant day when a resurrection would take place (John 11:24).

Jesus corrected her. He said, "I am [myself] the resurrection and the Life. Whoever believes in—adheres to, trusts in and relies on—me, although he may die, yet he shall live. And whoever continues to live and believe—has faith in, cleaves to and relies—on me shall never [actually] die at all" (John 11:25,26).

"Do you believe this?" Jesus asked Martha.

"Yes, Lord; I believe that you are the Christ, the Son of God, he who is coming into the world" (John 11:27). Martha did not understand all about this resurrection teaching, but one thing she knew for sure, Jesus Christ is the Son of God. He is the promised One. This she knew and this satisfied her. Do you know this? Are you satisfied by this truth about Jesus Christ? (Read John 3:16,17, Revelation 3:20.)

In this passage Jesus used another one of His famous "I AM's," as He said, "I am the resurrection, and the life: he that believeth in me, though he were dead, yet shall he live: and whosoever liveth and believeth in me shall never die" (John 11:25). He once more claimed to be God. But He was not finished yet. He now sent Martha to get her sister, Mary (John 11:28).

Jesus Wept

Mary left the house immediately. If the Lord Jesus wanted her, that was enough for her. She was ready to obey His command. The Jewish people saw Mary leave and followed her. When she came to where Jesus was, she fell at His feet. Martha believed in the Lord Jesus. She acknowledged it.

Mary believed, too. She showed it. She repeated the same words that Martha had said (John 11:21; John 11:32), "Lord, if you had been here, my brother would not have died." But there must have been a difference in the way she said them. Martha was a little disturbed because Jesus had not come immediately. Mary was only acknowledging her belief. If Jesus had been there Lazarus would not have died. She was right. Jesus said as much in John 11:15.

When the Lord Jesus heard the words of Mary and saw her sorrow and that of the Jews who were with her, He was deeply moved. The Lord realized more than anyone else that the sorrow was the result of sin and death. "Where have ye laid him?" Jesus asked.

The people led Him to the cave where Lazarus was buried (John 11:34). Jesus walked to the place and "He wept" (John 11:35). The

Jewish people saw the sorrow of the Lord and remarked at the love Jesus had for Lazarus (John 11:36). The Lord Jesus was moved with compassion when He saw the sorrow and the unbelief (John 11:33).

In some cultures today men are taught that it is wrong to weep, and yet the Lord Jesus Christ wept on this day. He wept at other times. In Luke 19:41 we read that, as He looked over the city of Jerusalem, He wept because of the people's unbelief.

As we trust the Holy Spirit to guide us moment-by-moment, the Lord will show us the times to laugh and the times to weep!

The Bible tells us that we are to weep with those who weep, and laugh with those who laugh (Romans 12:15). In the Old Testament we are told there is "a time to weep, and a time to laugh; a time to mourn, and a time to dance" (Ecclesiastes 3:4). As we trust the Holy Spirit to guide us moment-by-moment, the Lord will show us the times to laugh and the times to weep!

TEARS

I wept this morning, Lord;
    I don't let myself do it often,
        wet tears,
        heart-wrenching tears,
        soul-searching tears.

They seemed to drain away my
    heartaches,
        tensions,
            discouragements,
                disappointments.

Why are we all afraid to weep, Lord?
    Is it our BRITTLE, HARD society?
        which has told us
            no wet tears!
            no heart-wrenching tears!
            no soul-searching tears!
            not allowed!

189

You wept, Lord,
    long, long ago.
        If you could weep,
            is it OK for me, too?

—Doris Greig

The Lord Jesus Raises Lazarus from the Dead John 11:38-44

The group walked to the tomb. The tombs were either natural caves or caves hewn out in the rock. In such a tomb usually eight shelves were cut into the rock, three on each side and two on the wall facing the entrance. The bodies were laid on these shelves. The tomb had no door, but across the opening of the tomb was a groove in which was set a great stone like a cartwheel. The stone was rolled across the entrance so that the cave was sealed.

Now the Lord Jesus took over with the authority of the Son of God. "Take ye away the stone," He commanded.

Martha reminded the Lord that Lazarus had been dead for four days; it was too late for the Lord to view the body of His friend. That seemed to be all that entered Martha's mind! Already she had forgotten the Lord's words, "I am the resurrection and the life." Jesus Christ reminded her (John 11:40) of these words.

The people obeyed the command of Christ; they rolled away the stone. Then the Lord prayed (John 11:41,42). The Lord Jesus had been in constant communion with God, His Father, all of the time. In order that the people at the tomb might know of this communion, He voiced His prayer aloud and thanked God for hearing Him.

Then what did He do? "When he had said this, Jesus called in a loud voice, 'Lazarus, come out!'" (John 11:43). A white-haired man once declared in a meeting that it was wise that the Lord called "Lazarus" before He said, "Come out," or the entire graveyard population of Bethany would have come out of their tombs to greet Him!

The resurrected man came out; his hands and feet bound in bandages and his face wrapped with a cloth! A miracle of God was accomplished through His Son the Lord Jesus. Lazarus had been in the tomb for four days and ordinarily the odor of death and decay would have been obvious (John 11:39).

The Lord Jesus said, "Loose him, and let him go." The long strips of cloth that bound the embalming spices tightly against his body and head would have smothered Lazarus if they had not unbound him immediately!

The Pharisees Plot to Kill Jesus
John 11:45-57

Many of the Jewish people saw what happened and believed in the Lord Jesus (John 11:45). For this reason John wrote his Gospel. He wanted all other generations after this to believe that Jesus is the Christ, the Son of God.

The news of the death and resurrection of Lazarus had the effect of a stone dropped in water, the ripples quickly spreading farther and farther, until word of the Lord's miracle reached the ears of those who were plotting to take Jesus' life—the Pharisees. The enemies of the Lord could not deny this latest sign. After all, Lazarus had been dead for four days. The funeral service had been completed. But now Lazarus lived.

With this evidence, the Sanhedrin met and said of Jesus, "This man doeth many miracles" (John 11:47). They knew that, if they let Him go on, the whole nation would turn to Him. That would anger their Roman rulers, and the Sanhedrin would then lose its place of authority.

Only one road seemed open to them. Caiaphas, the high priest that year, stated it this way: "Nor do you understand or reason out that it is expedient and better for your own welfare that one man should die on behalf of the people than that the whole nation should perish (be destroyed, ruined)" (John 11:50). The high priest went on to say that the Lord Jesus should die for that nation (John 11:51). Caiaphas voiced terrible words, but all present agreed with him.

John notes that the words of Caiaphas were truer than he realized. He was right that Jesus Christ would give His life for the world, but Caiaphas did not realize what he had said. "He did not say this simply of his own accord" (John 11:51).

The hatred for the Lord Jesus had reached its peak. "Then from that day forth they took counsel together for to put him to death" (John 11:53). To them, they had no alternative but to do away with Him. And it was now only a matter of time until they did so, for the decision to destroy Him had been made.

Aware of the plot against Him, Jesus with His disciples left the vicinity of Jerusalem and went into a region near the wilderness to the city of Ephraim (John 11:54), until He was ready to lay down His life. His going away was not because He was afraid; he did it as a matter of strategy. He wanted to avoid open conflict because the time had not yet come, in the will of God, for Him to be shown to the people.

Back in Jerusalem, as crowds began arriving for the Passover, the people were looking for Jesus. They wondered if He would come to the feast. Expecting Him among the worshipers at the Temple, the chief priests and Pharisees gave strict orders that if anyone saw Him, they were to be informed, so they could arrest Him (John 11:55-57).

"Six days before the Passover ceremonies began, Jesus arrived in Bethany where Lazarus was—the man he had brought back to life. A banquet was prepared in Jesus' honor. Martha served, and Lazarus sat at the table with him. Then Mary took a jar of costly perfume made from essence of nard, and anointed Jesus' feet with it and wiped them with her hair. And the house was filled with fragrance" (John 12:1-3). This was Jesus' last supper at Bethany with His friends Mary, Martha and Lazarus. He indicated He would not be with them very long.

In Part II of the Gospel of John we will study Jesus' final days on earth, His Crucifixion and His Resurrection.